Fifth Named Entity Workshop

(NEWS 2015)

AA005212

Co-located with ACL-IJCNLP 2015

Beijing, China
31 July 2015

Editors:

Xiangyu Duan
Rafael E. Banchs
A. Kumara
Min Zhang
Haizhou Li

ISBN: 978-1-5108-0950-5

Printed from e-media with permission by:

Curran Associates, Inc.
57 Morehouse Lane
Red Hook, NY 12571

Some format issues inherent in the e-media version may also appear in this print version.

Copyright© (2015) by the Association for Computational Linguistics
All rights reserved.

Printed by Curran Associates, Inc. (2015)

For permission requests, please contact the Association for Computational Linguistics
at the address below.

Association for Computational Linguistics
209 N. Eighth Street
Stroudsburg, Pennsylvania 18360

Phone: 1-570-476-8006
Fax: 1-570-476-0860

acl@aclweb.org

Additional copies of this publication are available from:

Curran Associates, Inc.
57 Morehouse Lane
Red Hook, NY 12571 USA
Phone: 845-758-0400
Fax: 845-758-2634
Email: curran@proceedings.com
Web: www.proceedings.com

ACL 2015

Proceedings of
NEWS 2015
The Fifth Named Entities Workshop

Xiangyu Duan, Rafael E. Banchs, Min Zhang, Haizhou Li, A. Kumara
(Editors)

July 31, 2015
Beijing, China

Preface

The workshop series, Named Entities WorkShop (NEWS), focus on research on all aspects of the Named Entities, such as, identifying and analyzing named entities, mining, translating and transliterating named entities, etc. The first of the NEWS workshops (NEWS 2009) was held as a part of ACL-IJCNLP 2009 conference in Singapore; the second one, NEWS 2010, was held as an ACL 2010 workshop in Uppsala, Sweden; the third one, NEWS 2011, was held as an IJCNLP 2011 workshop in Chiang Mai, Thailand; and the fourth one, NEWS 2012, was held as an ACL 2012 workshop in Jeju, Korea. The current edition, NEWS 2015, was held as an ACL-IJCNLP 2015 workshop in Beijing, China.

The purpose of the NEWS workshop series is to bring together researchers across the world interested in identification, analysis, extraction, mining and transformation of named entities in monolingual or multilingual natural language text corpora. The workshop scope includes many interesting specific research areas pertaining to the named entities, such as, orthographic and phonetic characteristics, corpus analysis, unsupervised and supervised named entities extraction in monolingual or multilingual corpus, transliteration modeling, and evaluation methodologies, to name a few. For this year edition, 5 research papers were submitted, each paper was reviewed by at least 2 reviewers from the program committee. The 5 papers were all chosen for publication, covering named entity recognition and machine transliteration, which applied various new trend methods such as deep neural networks and graph-based semi-supervised learning.

Following the tradition of the NEWS workshop series, NEWS 2015 continued the machine transliteration shared task this year as well. The shared task was first introduced in NEWS 2009 and continued in NEWS 2010, NEWS 2011, and NEWS 2012. In NEWS 2015, by leveraging on the previous success of NEWS workshop series, we released the hand-crafted parallel named entities corpora to include 14 different language pairs from 12 language families, and made them available as the common dataset for the shared task. In total, 7 international teams participated from around the globe, while one team withdrew their results at the evaluation phase. Finally, we received 6 teams' submissions. The approaches ranged from traditional learning methods (such as, Phrasal SMT-based, Conditional Random Fields, etc.) to somewhat new approaches (such as, neural network transduction, integration of transliteration mining, hybrid system combination). A concrete study and targeted process between two languages often generate better performances. A report of the shared task that summarizes all submissions and the original whitepaper are also included in the proceedings, and will be presented in the workshop. The participants in the shared task were asked to submit short system papers (4 content pages each) describing their approaches, and each of such papers was reviewed by at least two members of the program committee to help improve the quality. All the 6 system papers were finally accepted to be published in the workshop proceedings.

We hope that NEWS 2015 would provide an exciting and productive forum for researchers working in this research area, and the NEWS-released data continues to serve as a standard dataset for machine transliteration generation and mining. We wish to thank all the researchers for their research submission and the enthusiastic participation in the transliteration shared tasks. We wish to express our gratitude to CJK Institute, Institute for Infocomm Research, Microsoft Research India, Thailand National Electronics and Computer Technology Centre and The Royal Melbourne Institute of Technology (RMIT)/Sarvnaz Karimi for preparing the data released as a part of the shared tasks. Finally, we thank all the program committee members for reviewing the submissions in spite of the tight schedule.

Workshop Organizers:
Min Zhang, Soochow University, China
Haizhou Li, Institute for Infocomm Research, Singapore
Rafael E Banchs, Institute for Infocomm Research, Singapore
A Kumaran, Microsoft Research, India
Xiangyu Duan, Soochow University, China

July 31, 2015
Beijing, China

Organizers:

Min Zhang, Soochow University, China
Haizhou Li, Institute for Infocomm Research, Singapore
Rafael E Banchs, Institute for Infocomm Research, Singapore
A Kumaran, Microsoft Research, India
Xiangyu Duan, Soochow University

Program Committee:

Rafael E. Banchs, Institute for Infocomm Research
Sivaji Bandyopadhyay, Jadavpur University
Marta R. Costa-jussà, Instituto Politécnico Nacional
Xiangyu Duan, Soochow University
Guohong Fu, Heilongjiang University
Sarvnaz Karimi, CSIRO
Mitesh M. Khapra, IBM Research India
Grzegorz Kondrak, University of Alberta
Jong-Hoon Oh, NICT
Richard Sproat, Google
Keh-Yih Su, Institute of Information Science, Academia Sinica
Raghavendra Udupa, Microsoft Research India
Chai Wutiwiwatchai, Intelligent Informatics Research Unit, National Electronics and Computer Technology Center
Deyi Xiong, Soochow University
Muyun Yang, Harbin Institute of Technology
Min Zhang, Soochow University

Table of Contents

Conference Program

Friday, July 31, 2015

9:05–9:15 ***Opening Remarks***

Whitepaper of NEWS 2015 Shared Task on Machine Transliteration
Min Zhang, Haizhou Li, Rafael E. Banchs and A. Kumaran

Report of NEWS 2015 Machine Transliteration Shared Task
Rafael E. Banchs, Min Zhang, Xiangyu Duan, Haizhou Li and A. Kumaran

9:15–10:05 ***Keynote Speech***

How do you spell that? A journey through word representations
Greg Kondrak

10:05–12:15 **Research Papers**

10:05–10:30 *Boosting Named Entity Recognition with Neural Character Embeddings*
Cicero dos Santos and Victor Guimarães

10:30–11:00 ***Coffee Break***

11:00–11:25 *Regularity and Flexibility in English-Chinese Name Transliteration*
Oi Yee Kwong

11:25–11:50 *HAREM and Klue: how to put two tagsets for named entities annotation together*
Livy Real and Alexandre Rademaker

11:50–12:15 *Semi-supervised Learning for Vietnamese Named Entity Recognition using Online Conditional Random Fields*
Quang Hong Pham, Minh-Le Nguyen, Thanh Binh Nguyen and Nguyen Viet Cuong

12:15–13:50 ***Lunch Break***

Friday, July 31, 2015 (continued)

13:50–16:50	**System Papers**
13:50–14:15	*Boosting English-Chinese Machine Transliteration via High Quality Alignment and Multilingual Resources* Yan Shao, Jörg Tiedemann and Joakim Nivre
14:15–14:40	*Neural Network Transduction Models in Transliteration Generation* Andrew Finch, Lemao Liu, Xiaolin Wang and Eiichiro Sumita
14:40–15:05	*A Hybrid Transliteration Model for Chinese/English Named Entities —BJTU-NLP Report for the 5th Named Entities Workshop* Dandan Wang, Xiaohui Yang, Jinan Xu, Yufeng Chen, Nan Wang, Bojia Liu, Jian Yang and Yujie Zhang
15:05–15:30	*Multiple System Combination for Transliteration* Garrett Nicolai, Bradley Hauer, Mohammad Salameh, Adam St Arnaud, Ying Xu, Lei Yao and Grzegorz Kondrak
15:30–16:00	***Coffee Break***
16:00–16:25	*Data representation methods and use of mined corpora for Indian language transliteration* Anoop Kunchukuttan and Pushpak Bhattacharyya
16:25–16:50	*NCU IISR English-Korean and English-Chinese Named Entity Transliteration Using Different Grapheme Segmentation Approaches* Yu-Chun Wang, Chun-Kai Wu and Richard Tzong-Han Tsai
16:50–17:00	**Closing**

Whitepaper of NEWS 2015 Shared Task on Machine Transliteration*

Min Zhang[⋆]**, Haizhou Li**[†]**, Rafael E. Banchs**[†]**, A Kumaran**[‡]

[⋆]Soochow University, China 215006
{minzhang}@suda.edu.cn

[†]Institute for Infocomm Research, A*STAR, Singapore 138632
{hli,rembanchs}@i2r.a-star.edu.sg

[‡]Multilingual Systems Research, Microsoft Research India
A.Kumaran@microsoft.com

Abstract

Transliteration is defined as phonetic translation of names across languages. Transliteration of Named Entities (NEs) is necessary in many applications, such as machine translation, corpus alignment, cross-language IR, information extraction and automatic lexicon acquisition. All such systems call for high-performance transliteration, which is the focus of shared task in the NEWS 2015 workshop. The objective of the shared task is to promote machine transliteration research by providing a common benchmarking platform for the community to evaluate the state-of-the-art technologies.

1 Task Description

The task is to develop machine transliteration system in one or more of the specified language pairs being considered for the task. Each language pair consists of a source and a target language. The training and development data sets released for each language pair are to be used for developing a transliteration system in whatever way that the participants find appropriate. At the evaluation time, a test set of source names only would be released, on which the participants are expected to produce a ranked list of transliteration candidates in another language (i.e. n-best transliterations), and this will be evaluated using common metrics. For every language pair the participants must submit at least one run that uses only the data provided by the NEWS workshop organisers in a given language pair (designated as "standard" run, primary submission). Users may submit more "stanrard" runs. They may also submit several "non-standard" runs for each language pair that use other data than those provided by the NEWS 2015 workshop; such runs would be evaluated and reported separately.

*http://translit.i2r.a-star.edu.sg/news2015/

2 Important Dates

Research paper submission deadline	14 May 2015
Shared task	
Registration opens	25 Feb 2015
Registration closes	25 April 2015
Training/Development data release	20 Feb 2015
Test data release	28 April 2015
Results Submission Due	4 May 2015
Results Announcement	9 May 2015
Task (short) Papers Due	14 May 2015
For all submissions	
Acceptance Notification	14 June 2015
Camera-Ready Copy Deadline	21 June 2015
Workshop Date	31 July 2015

3 Participation

1. Registration (15 Feb 2015)
   (a) NEWS Shared Task opens for registration.
   (b) Prospective participants are to register to the NEWS Workshop homepage.
2. Training & Development Data (20 Feb 2015)
   (a) Registered participants are to obtain training and development data from the Shared Task organiser and/or the designated copyright owners of databases.
   (b) All registered participants are required to participate in the evaluation of at least one language pair, submit the results and a short paper and attend the workshop at ACL-IJCNLP 2015.
3. Test data (28 April 2015)

Proceedings of the Fifth Named Entity Workshop, joint with 53rd ACL and the 7th IJCNLP, pages 1–9,
Beijing, China, July 26-31, 2015. ©2015 Association for Computational Linguistics

(a) The test data would be released on 28 April 2015, and the participants have a maximum of 5 days to submit their results in the expected format.

(b) One "standard" run must be submitted from every group on a given language pair. Additional "standard" runs may be submitted, up to 4 "standard" runs in total. However, the participants must indicate one of the submitted "standard" runs as the "primary submission". The primary submission will be used for the performance summary. In addition to the "standard" runs, more "non-standard" runs may be submitted. In total, maximum 8 runs (up to 4 "standard" runs plus up to 4 "non-standard" runs) can be submitted from each group on a registered language pair. The definition of "standard" and "non-standard" runs is in Section 5.

(c) Any runs that are "non-standard" must be tagged as such.

(d) The test set is a list of names in source language only. Every group will produce and submit a ranked list of transliteration candidates in another language for each given name in the test set. Please note that this shared task is a "transliteration generation" task, i.e., given a name in a source language one is supposed to generate one or more transliterations in a target language. It is not the task of "transliteration discovery", i.e., given a name in the source language and a set of names in the target language evaluate how to find the appropriate names from the target set that are transliterations of the given source name.

4. Results (4 May 2015)

(a) On 4 May 2015, the evaluation results would be announced and will be made available on the Workshop website.

(b) Note that only the scores (in respective metrics) of the participating systems on each language pairs would be published, and no explicit ranking of the participating systems would be published.

(c) Note that this is a shared evaluation task and not a competition; the results are meant to be used to evaluate systems on common data set with common metrics, and not to rank the participating systems. While the participants can cite the performance of their systems (scores on metrics) from the workshop report, they should not use any ranking information in their publications.

(d) Furthermore, all participants should agree not to reveal identities of other participants in any of their publications unless you get permission from the other respective participants. By default, all participants remain anonymous in published results, unless they indicate otherwise at the time of uploading their results. Note that the results of all systems will be published, but the identities of those participants that choose not to disclose their identity to other participants will be masked. As a result, in this case, your organisation name will still appear in the web site as one of participants, but it will not be linked explicitly to your results.

5. Short Papers on Task (14 May 2015)

(a) Each submitting site is required to submit a 4-page system paper (short paper) for its submissions, including their approach, data used and the results on either test set or development set or by n-fold cross validation on training set.

(b) The review of the system papers will be done to improve paper quality and readability and make sure the authors' ideas and methods can be understood by the workshop participants. We are aiming at accepting all system papers, and selected ones will be presented orally in the NEWS 2015 workshop.

(c) All registered participants are required to register and attend the workshop to introduce your work.

(d) All paper submission and review will be managed electronically through https://www.softconf.com/acl2015/news2015/.

4 Language Pairs

The tasks are to transliterate personal names or place names from a source to a target language as summarised in Table 1. NEWS 2015 Shared Task offers 14 evaluation subtasks, among them ChEn and ThEn are the back-transliteration of EnCh and EnTh tasks respectively. NEWS 2015 releases training, development and testing data for each of the language pairs. NEWS 2015 continues all language pairs that were evaluated in NEWS 2011 and 2012. In such cases, the training, development and test data in the release of NEWS 2015 are the same as those in NEWS 2012.

Please note that in order to have an accurate study of the research progress of machine translation technology, different from previous practice, the test/reference sets of NEWS 2011 are not released to the research community. Instead, we use the test sets of NEWS 2011 as progress test sets in NEWS 2015. NEWS 2015 participants are requested to submit results on the NEWS 2015 progress test sets (i.e., NEWS 2011 test sets). By doing so, we would like to do comparison studies by comparing the NEWS 2015 and NEWS 2011 results on the progress test sets and the NEWS 2015 and NEWS 2012 results on the test sets. We hope that we can have some insightful research findings in the progress studies.

The names given in the training sets for Chinese, Japanese, Korean, Thai and Persian languages are Western names and their respective transliterations; the Japanese Name (in English) → Japanese Kanji data set consists only of native Japanese names; the Arabic data set consists only of native Arabic names. The Indic data set (Hindi, Tamil, Kannada, Bangla) consists of a mix of Indian and Western names.

Examples of transliteration:

English → Chinese
Timothy → 蒂莫西

English → Japanese Katakana
Harrington → ハリントン

English → Korean Hangul
Bennett → 베넷

Japanese name in English → Japanese Kanji
Akihiro → 秋宏

English → Hindi
San Francisco → सैन फ्रान्सिस्को

English → Tamil
London → லண்டன்

English → Kannada
Tokyo → ಟೋಕ್ಯೋ

Arabic → Arabic name in English
خالد → Khalid

5 Standard Databases

Training Data (Parallel)
Paired names between source and target languages; size 7K – 37K.
Training Data is used for training a basic transliteration system.

Development Data (Parallel)
Paired names between source and target languages; size 1K – 2.8K.
Development Data is in addition to the Training data, which is used for system fine-tuning of parameters in case of need. Participants are allowed to use it as part of training data.

Testing Data
Source names only; size 1K – 2K.
This is a held-out set, which would be used for evaluating the quality of the transliterations.

Progress Testing Data
Source names only; size 0.6K – 2.6K.
This is the NEWS 2011 test set, it is held-out for progress study.

1. Participants will need to obtain licenses from the respective copyright owners and/or agree to the terms and conditions of use that are given on the downloading website (Li et al., 2004; MSRI, 2010; CJKI, 2010). NEWS 2015 will provide the contact details of each individual database. The data would be provided in Unicode UTF-8 encoding, in XML format; the results are expected to be submitted in UTF-8 encoding in XML format. The XML formats details are available in Appendix A.

2. The data are provided in 3 sets as described above.

3. Name pairs are distributed as-is, as provided by the respective creators.

Name origin	Source script	Target script	Data Owner	Data Size				Task ID
				Train	Dev	Progress Test	2012/2015 Test	
Western	English	Chinese	Institute for Infocomm Research	37K	2.8K	2K	1K	EnCh
Western	Chinese	English	Institute for Infocomm Research	28K	2.7K	2.2K	1K	ChEn
Western	English	Korean Hangul	CJK Institute	7K	1K	609	1K	EnKo
Western	English	Japanese Katakana	CJK Institute	26K	2K	1.8K	1K	EnJa
Japanese	English	Japanese Kanji	CJK Institute	10K	2K	571	1K	JnJk
Arabic	Arabic	English	CJK Institute	27K	2.5K	2.6K	1K	ArEn
Mixed	English	Hindi	Microsoft Research India	12K	1K	1K	1K	EnHi
Mixed	English	Tamil	Microsoft Research India	10K	1K	1K	1K	EnTa
Mixed	English	Kannada	Microsoft Research India	10K	1K	1K	1K	EnKa
Mixed	English	Bangla	Microsoft Research India	13K	1K	1K	1K	EnBa
Western	English	Thai	NECTEC	27K	2K	2K	1K	EnTh
Western	Thai	English	NECTEC	25K	2K	1.9K	1K	ThEn
Western	English	Persian	Sarvnaz Karimi / RMIT	10K	2K	2K	1K	EnPe
Western	English	Hebrew	Microsoft Research India	9.5K	1K	1K	1K	EnHe

Table 1: Source and target languages for the shared task on transliteration.

(a) While the databases are mostly manually checked, there may be still inconsistency (that is, non-standard usage, region-specific usage, errors, etc.) or incompleteness (that is, not all right variations may be covered).

(b) The participants may use any method to further clean up the data provided.

i. If they are cleaned up manually, we appeal that such data be provided back to the organisers for redistribution to all the participating groups in that language pair; such sharing benefits all participants, and further ensures that the evaluation provides normalisation with respect to data quality.

ii. If automatic cleanup were used, such cleanup would be considered a part of the system fielded, and hence not required to be shared with all participants.

4. *Standard Runs* We expect that the participants to use only the data (parallel names) provided by the Shared Task for transliteration task for a "standard" run to ensure a fair evaluation. One such run (using only the data provided by the shared task) is mandatory for all participants for a given language pair that they participate in.

5. *Non-standard Runs* If more data (either parallel names data or monolingual data) were used, then all such runs using extra data must be marked as "non-standard". For such "non-standard" runs, it is required to disclose the size and characteristics of the data used in the system paper.

6. A participant may submit a maximum of 8 runs for a given language pair (including the mandatory 1 "standard" run marked as "primary submission").

6 Paper Format

Paper submissions to NEWS 2015 should follow the ACL 2015 paper submission policy, including paper format, blind review policy and title and author format convention. Full papers (research paper) are in two-column format without exceeding eight (8) pages of content plus two (2) extra page for references and short papers (task paper) are also in two-column format without exceeding four (4) pages content plus two (2) extra page for references. Submission must conform to the official ACL 2015 style guidelines. For details, please refer to the ACL 2015 website[2].

7 Evaluation Metrics

We plan to measure the quality of the transliteration task using the following 4 metrics. We accept up to 10 output candidates in a ranked list for each input entry.

Since a given source name may have multiple correct target transliterations, all these alternatives are treated equally in the evaluation. That is, any of these alternatives are considered as a correct

[2] http://www.ACL2015.org/

transliteration, and the first correct transliteration in the ranked list is accepted as a correct hit.

The following notation is further assumed:

N	:	Total number of names (source words) in the test set
n_i	:	Number of reference transliterations for i-th name in the test set ($n_i \geq 1$)
$r_{i,j}$	:	j-th reference transliteration for i-th name in the test set
$c_{i,k}$	:	k-th candidate transliteration (system output) for i-th name in the test set ($1 \leq k \leq 10$)
K_i	:	Number of candidate transliterations produced by a transliteration system

1. Word Accuracy in Top-1 (ACC) Also known as Word Error Rate, it measures correctness of the first transliteration candidate in the candidate list produced by a transliteration system. $ACC = 1$ means that all top candidates are correct transliterations i.e. they match one of the references, and $ACC = 0$ means that none of the top candidates are correct.

$$ACC = \frac{1}{N}\sum_{i=1}^{N}\left\{\begin{array}{l}1 \text{ if } \exists\, r_{i,j} : r_{i,j} = c_{i,1};\\ 0 \text{ otherwise}\end{array}\right\} \quad (1)$$

2. Fuzziness in Top-1 (Mean F-score) The mean F-score measures how different, on average, the top transliteration candidate is from its closest reference. F-score for each source word is a function of Precision and Recall and equals 1 when the top candidate matches one of the references, and 0 when there are no common characters between the candidate and any of the references.

Precision and Recall are calculated based on the length of the Longest Common Subsequence between a candidate and a reference:

$$LCS(c, r) = \frac{1}{2}\left(|c| + |r| - ED(c, r)\right) \quad (2)$$

where ED is the edit distance and $|x|$ is the length of x. For example, the longest common subsequence between "abcd" and "afcde" is "acd" and its length is 3. The best matching reference, that is, the reference for which the edit distance has the minimum, is taken for calculation. If the best matching reference is given by

$$r_{i,m} = \arg\min_j \left(ED(c_{i,1}, r_{i,j})\right) \quad (3)$$

then Recall, Precision and F-score for i-th word are calculated as

$$R_i = \frac{LCS(c_{i,1}, r_{i,m})}{|r_{i,m}|} \quad (4)$$

$$P_i = \frac{LCS(c_{i,1}, r_{i,m})}{|c_{i,1}|} \quad (5)$$

$$F_i = 2\frac{R_i \times P_i}{R_i + P_i} \quad (6)$$

- The length is computed in distinct Unicode characters.
- No distinction is made on different character types of a language (e.g., vowel vs. consonants vs. combining diereses' etc.)

3. Mean Reciprocal Rank (MRR) Measures traditional MRR *for any right answer* produced by the system, from among the candidates. $1/MRR$ tells approximately the average rank of the correct transliteration. MRR closer to 1 implies that the correct answer is mostly produced close to the top of the n-best lists.

$$RR_i = \left\{\begin{array}{l}\min_j \frac{1}{j} \text{ if } \exists r_{i,j}, c_{i,k} : r_{i,j} = c_{i,k};\\ 0 \text{ otherwise}\end{array}\right\} \quad (7)$$

$$MRR = \frac{1}{N}\sum_{i=1}^{N} RR_i \quad (8)$$

4. MAP$_{ref}$ Measures tightly the precision in the n-best candidates for i-th source name, for which reference transliterations are available. If all of the references are produced, then the MAP is 1. Let's denote the number of correct candidates for the i-th source word in k-best list as $num(i, k)$. MAP$_{ref}$ is then given by

$$MAP_{ref} = \frac{1}{N}\sum_{i}^{N}\frac{1}{n_i}\left(\sum_{k=1}^{n_i} num(i, k)\right) \quad (9)$$

8 Contact Us

If you have any questions about this share task and the database, please email to

Dr. Rafael E. Banchs
Institute for Infocomm Research (I^{2}R), A*STAR
1 Fusionopolis Way
#08-05 South Tower, Connexis
Singapore 138632
rembanchs@i2r.a-star.edu.sg

Dr. Min Zhang
Soochow University
China 215006
zhangminmt@hotmail.com

References

[CJKI2010] CJKI. 2010. CJK Institute. http://www.cjk.org/.

[Li et al.2004] Haizhou Li, Min Zhang, and Jian Su. 2004. A joint source-channel model for machine transliteration. In *Proc. 42nd ACL Annual Meeting*, pages 159–166, Barcelona, Spain.

[MSRI2010] MSRI. 2010. Microsoft Research India. http://research.microsoft.com/india.

A Training/Development Data

- File Naming Conventions:
  `NEWS12_train_XXYY_nnnn.xml`
  `NEWS12_dev_XXYY_nnnn.xml`
  `NEWS12_test_XXYY_nnnn.xml`
  `NEWS11_test_XXYY_nnnn.xml`
  `(progress test sets)`
  - `XX`: Source Language
  - `YY`: Target Language
  - `nnnn`: size of parallel/monolingual names ("25K", "10000", etc)

- File formats:
  All data will be made available in XML formats (Figure 1).

- Data Encoding Formats:
  The data will be in Unicode UTF-8 encoding files without byte-order mark, and in the XML format specified.

B Submission of Results

- File Naming Conventions:
  You can give your files any name you like. During submission online you will need to indicate whether this submission belongs to a "standard" or "non-standard" run, and if it is a "standard" run, whether it is the primary submission.

- File formats:
  All data will be made available in XML formats (Figure 2).

- Data Encoding Formats:
  The results are expected to be submitted in UTF-8 encoded files without byte-order mark only, and in the XML format specified.

```
<?xml version="1.0" encoding="UTF-8"?>

<TransliterationCorpus
    CorpusID = "NEWS2012-Train-EnHi-25K"
    SourceLang = "English"
    TargetLang = "Hindi"
    CorpusType = "Train|Dev"
    CorpusSize = "25000"
    CorpusFormat = "UTF8">

    <Name ID=" 1" >
        <SourceName>eeeeee1</SourceName>
        <TargetName ID="1">hhhhhh1_1</TargetName>
            <TargetName ID="2">hhhhhh1_2</TargetName>
        ...
        <TargetName ID="n">hhhhhh1_n</TargetName>
    </Name>
    <Name ID=" 2" >
        <SourceName>eeeeee2</SourceName>
        <TargetName ID="1">hhhhhh2_1</TargetName>
        <TargetName ID="2">hhhhhh2_2</TargetName>
        ...
        <TargetName ID="m">hhhhhh2_m</TargetName>
    </Name>
    ...
    <!-- rest of the names to follow -->
    ...
</TransliterationCorpus>
```

Figure 1: File: NEWS2012_Train_EnHi_25K.xml

```xml
<?xml version="1.0" encoding="UTF-8"?>

<TransliterationTaskResults
    SourceLang = "English"
    TargetLang = "Hindi"
    GroupID = "Trans University"
    RunID = "1"
    RunType = "Standard"
    Comments = "HMM Run with params: alpha=0.8 beta=1.25">

    <Name ID="1">
        <SourceName>eeeeee1</SourceName>
        <TargetName ID="1">hhhhhh11</TargetName>
        <TargetName ID="2">hhhhhh12</TargetName>
        <TargetName ID="3">hhhhhh13</TargetName>
        ...
        <TargetName ID="10">hhhhhh110</TargetName>

        <!-- Participants to provide their
        top 10 candidate transliterations -->
    </Name>
    <Name ID="2">
        <SourceName>eeeeee2</SourceName>
        <TargetName ID="1">hhhhhh21</TargetName>
        <TargetName ID="2">hhhhhh22</TargetName>
        <TargetName ID="3">hhhhhh23</TargetName>
        ...
        <TargetName ID="10">hhhhhh110</TargetName>
        <!-- Participants to provide their
        top 10 candidate transliterations -->
    </Name>
    ...
    <!-- All names in test corpus to follow -->
    ...
</TransliterationTaskResults>
```

Figure 2: Example file: NEWS2012_EnHi_TUniv_01_StdRunHMMBased.xml

Report of NEWS 2015 Machine Transliteration Shared Task

Rafael E. Banchs[1], Min Zhang[2], Xiangyu Duan[2], Haizhou Li[1], A. Kumaran[3]
[1] Institute for Infocomm Research, A*STAR, Singapore 138632
{rembanchs,hli}@i2r.a-star.edu.sg
[2] Soochow University, China 215006
{minzhang,xiangyuduan}@suda.edu.cn
[3]Multilingual Systems Research, Microsoft Research India
a.kumaran@microsoft.com

Abstract

This report presents the results from the Machine Transliteration Shared Task conducted as part of The Fifth Named Entities Workshop (NEWS 2015) held at ACL 2015 in Beijing, China. Similar to previous editions of NEWS Workshop, the Shared Task featured machine transliteration of proper names over 14 different language pairs, including 12 different languages and two different Japanese scripts. A total of 6 teams participated in the evaluation, submitting 194 standard and 12 non-standard runs, involving a diverse variety of transliteration methodologies. Four performance metrics were used to report the evaluation results. Once again, the NEWS shared task on machine transliteration has successfully achieved its objectives by providing a common ground for the research community to conduct comparative evaluations of state-of-the-art technologies that will benefit the future research and development in this area.

1 Introduction

Names play an important role in the performance of most Natural Language Processing (NLP) and Information Retrieval (IR) applications. They are also critical in cross-lingual applications such as Machine Translation (MT) and Cross-language Information Retrieval (CLIR), as it has been shown that system performance correlates positively with the quality of name conversion across languages (Demner-Fushman and Oard 2002, Mandl and Womser-Hacker 2005, Hermjakob et al. 2008, Udupa et al. 2009). Bilingual dictionaries constitute the traditional source of information for name conversion across languages, however they offer very limited support due to the fact that, in most languages, names are continuously emerging and evolving.

All of the above points to the critical need for robust Machine Transliteration methods and systems. During the last decade, significant efforts has been conducted by the research community to address the problem of machine transliteration (Knight and Graehl 1998, Meng et al. 2001, Li et al. 2004, Zelenko and Aone 2006, Sproat et al. 2006, Sherif and Kondrak 2007, Hermjakob et al. 2008, Al-Onaizan and Knight 2002, Goldwasser and Roth 2008, Goldberg and Elhadad 2008, Klementiev and Roth 2006, Oh and Choi 2002, Virga and Khudanpur 2003, Wan and Verspoor 1998, Kang and Choi 2000, Gao et al. 2004, Li et al. 2009a, Li et al. 2009b). These previous works fall into three main categories: grapheme-based, phoneme-based and hybrid methods. Grapheme based methods (Li et al. 2004) treat transliteration as a direct orthographic mapping and only uses orthography-related features while phoneme-based methods (Knight and Graehl 1998) make use of phonetic correspondences to generate the transliteration. The hybrid approach refers to the combination of several different models or knowledge sources to support the transliteration generation process.

The first machine transliteration shared task (Li et al. 2009b, Li et al. 2009a) was organized and conducted as part of NEWS 2009 at ACL-IJCNLP 2009. It was the first time that common benchmarking data in diverse language pairs was provided for evaluating state-of-the-art machine transliteration. While the focus of the 2009 shared task was on establishing the quality metrics and on setting up a baseline for transliteration quality based on those metrics, the 2010 shared task (Li et al. 2010a, Li et al. 2010b) focused on expanding the scope of the transliteration generation task to about a dozen languages and on exploring the quality of the task depending on the direction of transliteration. In NEWS 2011 (Zhang et al. 2011a, Zhang et al. 2011b),

Proceedings of the Fifth Named Entity Workshop, joint with 53rd ACL and the 7th IJCNLP, pages 10–23,
Beijing, China, July 26-31, 2015. ©2015 Association for Computational Linguistics

the focus was on significantly increasing the hand-crafted parallel corpora of named entities to include 14 different language pairs from 11 language families, and on making them available as the common dataset for the shared task. The NEWS 2015 Shared Task on Transliteration has been a continued effort for evaluating machine transliteration performance over such a common dataset following the NEWS 2012 (Zhang et al. 2012) and 2011 shared tasks.

In this paper, we present in full detail the results of the NEWS 2015 Machine Transliteration Shared Task. The rest of the paper is structured as follows. Section 2 provides as short review of the main characteristics of the machine transliteration task and the corpora used for it. Section 3 reviews the four metrics used for the evaluations. Section 4 reports specific details about participation in the 2015 edition of the shared task, and section 5 presents and discusses the evaluation results. Finally, section 6 presents our main conclusions and future plans.

2 Shared Task on Transliteration

Transliteration, sometimes also called Romanization, especially if Latin Scripts are used for target strings (Halpern 2007), deals with the conversion of names between two languages and/or script systems. Within the context of the Transliteration Shared Task, we are aiming not only at addressing the name conversion process but also its practical utility for downstream applications, such as MT and CLIR.

In this sense, we adopt the same definition of transliteration as proposed during the NEWS 2009 workshop (Li et al. 2009a). According to it, transliteration is understood as the "conversion of a given name in the source language (a text string in the source writing system or orthography) to a name in the target language (another text string in the target writing system or orthography" conditioned to the following specific requirements regarding the name representation in the target language:

- it is phonetically equivalent to the source name,
- it conforms to the phonology of the target language, and
- it matches the user intuition on its equivalence with respect to the source language name.

Following NEWS 2011 and NEWS 2012, the three back-transliteration tasks are maintained. Back-transliteration attempts to restore transliterated names back into their original source language. For instance, the tasks for converting western names written in Chinese and Thai back into their original English spellings are considered. Similarly, a task for back-transliterating Romanized Japanese names into their original Kanji strings is considered too.

2.1 Shared Task Description

Following the tradition of NEWS workshop series, the shared task in NEWS 2015 consists of developing machine transliteration systems in one or more of the specified language pairs. Each language pair of the shared task consists of a source and a target language, implicitly specifying the transliteration direction. Training and development data in each of the language pairs was made available to all registered participants for developing their transliteration systems.

At the evaluation time, a standard hand-crafted test set consisting of between 500 and 3,000 source names (approximately 5-10% of the training data size) was released, on which the participants were required to produce a ranked list of transliteration candidates in the target language for each source name. The system output is tested against a reference set (which may include multiple correct transliterations for some source names), and the performance of a system is captured in multiple metrics (defined in Section 3), each designed to capture a specific performance dimension.

For every language pair, each participant was required to submit at least one run (designated as a "standard" run) that uses only the data provided by the NEWS workshop organizers in that language pair; i.e. no other data or linguistic resources are allowed for standard runs. This ensures parity between systems and enables meaningful comparison of performance of various algorithmic approaches in a given language pair. Participants were allowed to submit one or more standard runs for each task they participated in. If more than one standard runs were submitted, it was required to name one of them as a "primary" run, which was the one used to compare results across different systems.

In addition, more than one "non-standard" runs could be submitted for every language pair using either data beyond the one provided by the shared task organizers, any other available linguistic resources in a specific language pair, or both. This essentially enabled participants to demonstrate the limits of performance of their systems in a given language pair.

2.2 Shared Task Corpora

Two specific constraints were considered when selecting languages for the shared task: language diversity and data availability. To make the shared task interesting and to attract wider participation, it is important to ensure a reasonable variety among the languages in terms of linguistic diversity, orthography and geography. Clearly, the ability of procuring and distributing a reasonably large (approximately 10K paired names for training and testing together) hand-crafted corpora consisting primarily of paired names is critical for this process. Following NEWS 2011, the 14 tasks shown in Tables 1.a-e were used (Li et al. 2004, Kumaran and Kellner 2007, MSRI 2009, CJKI 2010). Additionally, the test sets from NEWS 2012 (each of size 1K) were also used for evaluation purposes in this shared task.

The names given in the training sets for Chinese, Japanese, Korean, Thai, Persian and Hebrew languages are Western names and their respective transliterations; the Japanese Name (in English) → Japanese Kanji data set consists only of native Japanese names; the Arabic data set consists only of native Arabic names. The Indic data set (Hindi, Tamil, Kannada, Bangla) consists of a mix of Indian and Western names.

For all of the tasks chosen, we have been able to procure paired-name data between the source and the target scripts and were able to make them available to the participants. For some language pairs, such as the case of English-Chinese and English-Thai, there are both transliteration and back-transliteration tasks. Most of the tasks are just one-way transliteration, although Indian data sets contains a mixture of names from both Indian and Western origins.

3 Evaluation Metrics and Rationale

The participants have been asked to submit standard and, optionally, non-standard runs. One of the standard runs must be named as the primary submission, which was the one used for the performance summary. Each run must contain a ranked list of up to ten candidate transliterations for each source name. The submitted results are compared to the ground truth (reference transliterations) using four evaluation metrics capturing different aspects of transliteration performance. The four considered evaluation metrics are:

- Word Accuracy in Top-1 (ACC),
- Fuzziness in Top-1 (Mean F-score),
- Mean Reciprocal Rank (MRR), and
- Mean Average Precision (MAP_{ref}).

Task ID: EnCh			*data size*		
Origin	*Source*	*Target*	*Train*	*Dev*	*Test*
Western	English	Chinese	37K	2.8K	2.0K
Task ID: ChEn			*data size*		
Origin	*Source*	*Target*	*Train*	*Dev*	*Test*
Western	Chinese	English	28K	2.7K	2.7K

Table 1.a: Datasets provided by Institute for Infocomm Research, Singapore.

Task ID: EnKo			*data size*		
Origin	*Source*	*Target*	*Train*	*Dev*	*Test*
Western	English	Korean	7.0K	1.0K	0.6K
Task ID: EnJa			*data size*		
Origin	*Source*	*Target*	*Train*	*Dev*	*Test*
Western	English	Katakana	26K	2.0K	1.8K
Task ID: JnJk			*data size*		
Origin	*Source*	*Target*	*Train*	*Dev*	*Test*
Japanese	English	Kanji	10K	2.0K	0.6K
Task ID: ArEn			*data size*		
Origin	*Source*	*Target*	*Train*	*Dev*	*Test*
Arabic	Arabic	English	27K	2.5K	2.6K

Table 1.b: Datasets provided by the CJK Institute, Japan.

Task ID: EnHi			*data size*		
Origin	*Source*	*Target*	*Train*	*Dev*	*Test*
Mixed	English	Hindi	12K	1.0K	1.0K
Task ID: EnTa			*data size*		
Origin	*Source*	*Target*	*Train*	*Dev*	*Test*
Mixed	English	Tamil	10K	1.0K	1.0K
Task ID: EnKa			*data size*		
Origin	*Source*	*Target*	*Train*	*Dev*	*Test*
Mixed	English	Kannada	10K	1.0K	1.0K
Task ID: EnBa			*data size*		
Origin	*Source*	*Target*	*Train*	*Dev*	*Test*
Mixed	English	Bangla	13K	1.0K	1.0K
Task ID: EnHe			*data size*		
Origin	*Source*	*Target*	*Train*	*Dev*	*Test*
Western	English	Hebrew	9.5K	1.0K	1.0K

Table 1.c: Datasets provided by Microsoft Research India.

Task ID: EnTh			*data size*		
Origin	*Source*	*Target*	*Train*	*Dev*	*Test*
Western	English	Thai	27K	2.0K	2.0K
Task ID: ThEn			*data size*		
Origin	*Source*	*Target*	*Train*	*Dev*	*Test*
Western	Thai	English	25K	2.0K	1.9K

Table 1.d: Datasets provided by National Electronics and Computer Technology Center.

Task ID: EnPe			*data size*		
Origin	*Source*	*Target*	*Train*	*Dev*	*Test*
Western	English	Persian	10K	2.0K	2.0K

Table 1.e: Dataset provided by Sarvnaz Karimi / RMIT.

In the next subsections, we present a brief description of the four considered evaluation metrics. The following notation is further assumed:

- N : Total number of names (source words) in the test set,
- n_i : Number of reference transliterations for i-th name in the test set ($n_i \geq 1$),
- $r_{i,j}$: j-th reference transliteration for i-th name in the test set,
- $c_{i,k}$: k-th candidate transliteration (system output) for i-th name in the test set ($1 \leq k \leq 10$),
- K_i : Number of candidate transliterations produced by a transliteration system.

3.1 Word Accuracy in Top-1 (ACC)

Also known as Word Error Rate, it measures correctness of the first transliteration candidate in the candidate list produced by a transliteration system. $ACC = 1$ means that all top candidates are correct transliterations; i.e. they match one of the references, and $ACC = 0$ means that none of the top candidates are correct.

$$ACC = \frac{1}{N}\sum_{i=1}^{N}\left\{\begin{matrix} 1\ if\ \exists r_{i,j} : r_{i,j} = c_{i,1}\ ; \\ 0\ otherwise \end{matrix}\right\} \qquad \text{(Eq.1)}$$

3.2 Fuzziness in Top-1 (Mean F-score)

The Mean F-score measures how different, on average, the top transliteration candidate is from its closest reference. F-score for each source word is a function of Precision and Recall and equals 1 when the top candidate matches one of the references, and 0 when there are no common characters between the candidate and any of the references.

Precision and Recall are calculated based on the length of the Longest Common Subsequence (LCS) between a candidate and a reference:

$$LCS(c,r) = \frac{1}{2}\left(|c| + |r| - ED(c,r)\right) \qquad \text{(Eq.2)}$$

where ED is the edit distance and $|x|$ is the length of x. For example, the longest common subsequence between "abcd" and "afcde" is "acd" and its length is 3. The best matching reference, i.e. the reference for which the edit distance has the minimum, is taken for calculation. If the best matching reference is given by

$$r_{i,m} = \arg min_j\left(ED\left(c_{i,1}, r_{i,j}\right)\right) \qquad \text{(Eq.3)}$$

the Recall, Precision and F-score for the i-th word are calculated as:

$$R_i = \frac{LCS(c_{i,1}, r_{i,m})}{|r_{i,m}|} \qquad \text{(Eq.4)}$$

$$P_i = \frac{LCS(c_{i,1}, r_{i,m})}{|c_{i,1}|} \qquad \text{(Eq.5)}$$

$$F_i = 2\frac{R_i \times P_i}{R_i + P_i} \qquad \text{(Eq.6)}$$

The lengths are computed with respect to distinct Unicode characters, and no distinctions are made for different character types of a language (e.g. vowel vs. consonant vs. combining diereses, etc.).

3.3 Mean Reciprocal Rank (MRR)

Measures traditional MRR for any right answer produced by the system, from among the candidates. 1/MRR tells approximately the average rank of the correct transliteration. MRR closer to 1 implies that the correct answer is mostly produced close to the top of the n-best lists.

$$RR_i = \left\{\begin{matrix} min_j \frac{1}{j}\ if\ \exists r_{i,j}, c_{i,k} : r_{i,j} = c_{i,k}\ ; \\ 0\ otherwise \end{matrix}\right\} \qquad \text{(Eq.7)}$$

$$MRR = \frac{1}{N}\sum_{i=1}^{N} RR_i \qquad \text{(Eq.8)}$$

3.4 Mean Average Precision (MAP_{ref})

This metric measures tightly the precision in the n-best candidates for i-th source name, for which reference transliterations are available. If all of the references are produced, then the MAP is 1. If we denote the number of correct candidates for the i-th source word in k-best list as $num(i,k)$, then MAP_{ref} is given by:

$$MAP_{ref} = \frac{1}{N}\sum_{i=1}^{N}\frac{1}{n_i}\left(\sum_{k=1}^{n_i} num(i,k)\right) \qquad \text{(Eq.9)}$$

4 Participation in the Shared Task

A total of six teams from six different institutions participated in the NEWS 2015 Shared Task. More specifically, the participating teams were from University of Alberta (UALB), Uppsala University (UPPS), Beijing Jiaotong University (BJTU), the National Institute of Information and Communications Technology (NICT), the Indian Institute of Technology Bombay (IITB) and the National Taiwan University (NTU).

Teams were required to submit at least one standard run for every task they participated in, and for both, NEWS 2011 and NEWS 2012, test sets. The former was used as a progress evaluation set and the latter as the official NEWS 2015 evaluation set. In total, we received 97 standard and 6 non-standard runs for each test set; i.e. 194 standard and 12 non-standard runs in total. Table 2 summarizes the number of standard runs, non-standard runs and teams participating per task.

Task	Std	Non	Teams Participating
EnCh	26	2	UALB, UPPS, BJTU, NICT, IITB, NTU
ChEn	20	2	UPPS, BJTU, NICT, IITB
EnKo	18	0	NICT, NTU
EnJa	6	0	UALB, NICT
JnJk	4	0	NICT
ArEn	6	0	UALB, NICT
EnHi	20	2	UALB, NICT, IITB
EnTa	20	2	UALB, NICT, IITB
EnKa	12	2	UALB, NICT, IITB
EnBa	18	0	UALB, NICT, IITB
EnHe	12	2	UALB, NICT, IITB
EnTh	10	0	UALB, NICT, IITB
ThEn	10	0	UALB, NICT, IITB
EnPe	12	0	UALB, NICT, IITB
	194	**12**	

Table 2: Number of standard (Std) and non-standard (Non) runs submitted, and teams participating in each task.

As seen from the table, the most popular task continues to be the transliteration from English to Chinese (Zhang et al. 2012), followed by Chinese to English, English to Hindi, and English to Tamil. Non-standard runs were only submitted for 6 of the 14 tasks.

5 Task Results and Analysis

Figure 1 summarizes the results of the NEWS 2015 Shared Task. In the figure, only F-scores over the NEWS 2012 evaluation test set (referred to as NEWS12/15) for all primary standard submissions are depicted. A total of 41 primary standard submissions were received.

As seen from the figure, with the exception of the English to Japanese Katakana, only transliteration tasks involving Arabic, Persian and the four considered Indian languages are consistently scored above 80%. For the rest of the languages, with the exception of Japanese Katakana and Hebrew, scores are consistently in the range from 60% to 80%. Notice also that, regardless the availability of training data, the English to Chinese transliteration task seems to be the more demanding one for state-of-the-art systems with respect to the considered metric.

Another interesting observation that can be derived from the figure, when looking to the language pairs English-Chinese and English-Thai, is that systems tend to perform slightly better for the case of back-transliteration tasks.

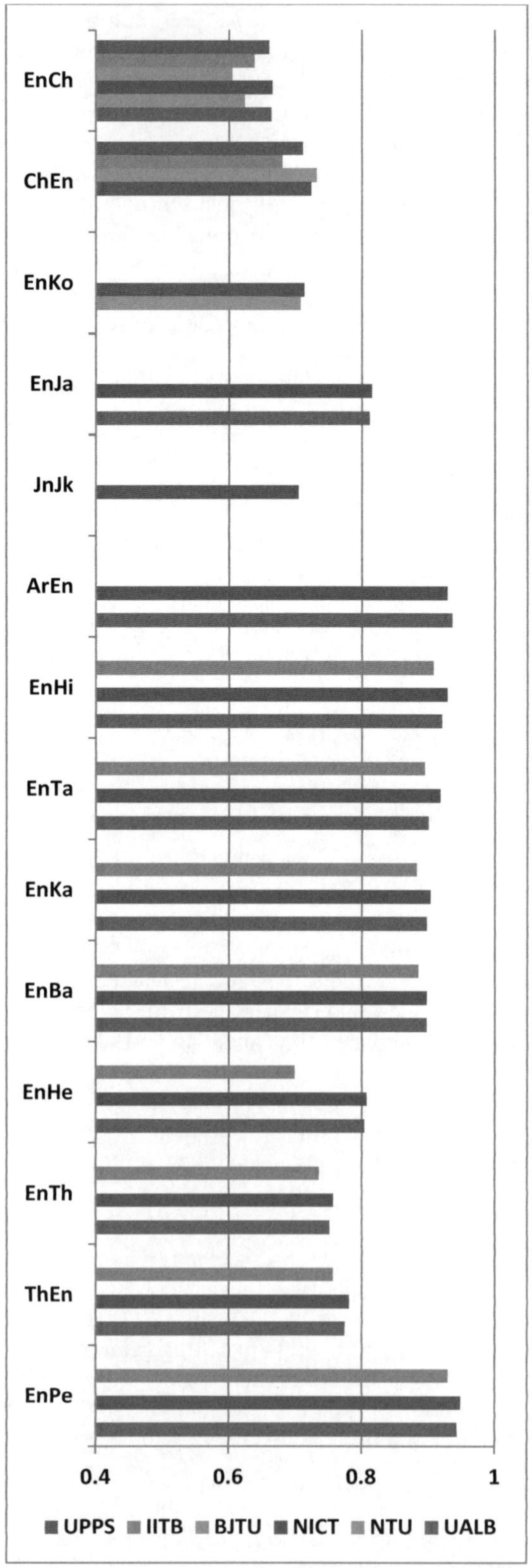

Figure 1: Mean F-scores (Top-1) on the evaluation test set (NEWS12/15) for all primary standard submissions and all transliteration tasks.

A much more comprehensive presentation of results for the NEWS 2015 Shared Task is provided in the Appendix at the end of this paper. There, resulting scores are reported for all received submissions, including standard and non-standard submissions, over both the progress test (NEWS11) and evaluation test (NEWS12/15), and the four considered evaluation metrics. All results are presented in 28 tables, each of which reports the scores for one transliteration task over one test set. In the tables, all primary standard runs are highlighted in bold-italic fonts.

Regarding the systems participating in this year evaluation, the UALB's system (Nicolai et al. 2015) was based on multiple system combinations. They presented experimental results involving three different well-known transliteration approaches: DirecTL+ (Jiampojamarn et al. 2009), Sequitur (Bisani and Ney 2008) and SMT (Koehn et al. 2007). They showed error reductions of up to 20% over a baseline system by using system combination.

The UPPS's system (Shao et al. 2015) implemented a phrase-based transliteration approach, which is enhanced with refined alignments produced by the M2M-aligner (Jiampojamarn et al. 2007). They also implemented a ranking mechanism based on a linear regression, showing a significant improvement on both EnCh and ChEn transliteration tasks.

The BJTU's system (Wang et al. 2015a) implemented an SMT (Koehn et al. 2007) log linear model combination for transliteration, including standard SMT features such as a language model scores and forward and reverse phrase translation probabilities, as well as other specific transliteration features such as length of names and length of name penalties.

The NICT's system (Finch et al. 2015) builds upon their previous SMT-based system used for NEWS 2012 (Finch et al. 2012). In this shared task, the previous system rescoring step is augmented with a neural network based transliteration model (Bahdanau et al. 2014). They showed significant improvements in 8 of the 14 transliteration tasks with respect to their 2012 system.

The ITTB's system (Kunchukuttan and Bhattacharyya 2015) also followed the SMT approach to transliteration. In this case they include two specific preprocessing enhancements: the addition of word-boundary markers, and a language-independent overlapping character segmentation. They observed that word-boundary markers substantially improved transliteration accuracy, and overlapping segmentation showed some potential.

The NTU's system (Wang et al. 2015b) is based on DirecTL+ with alignments generated by the M2M-aligner (Jiampojamarn et al. 2010). In preprocessing, they experimented with different grapheme segmentation methods for English, Chinese and Korean; while in post-processing, they evaluated two re-ranking approaches: orthography similarity ranking and web-based ranking.

As seen from the previous system descriptions, phrase-based SMT approaches are still predominant in the state-of-the-art for machine transliteration. Significant improvements are achieved by incorporating novel approaches in the preprocessing and post-processing stages, as well as by system combinations. Regarding pre-processing, the main focus was on segmentation, while in post-processing, using neural networks for rescoring provided the most significant gains.

Finally, figure 2 compares, in terms of Mean F-scores, the best primary standard submissions in NEWS 2012 with the ones in NEWS 2015.

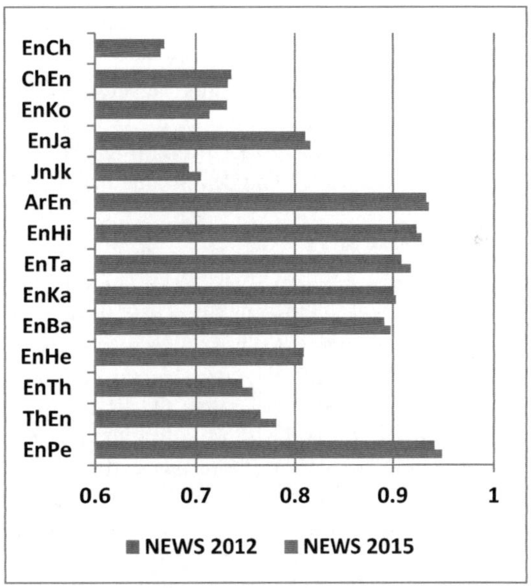

Figure 2: Mean F-scores (Top-1) on the evaluation test set (NEWS12/15) for the best primary standard submissions in 2012 and 2015.

As seen from the figure, in most of the considered transliteration tasks, some incremental improvements can be observed between the 2012 and 2015 shared tasks. The most significant improvements are in those tasks involving Japanese Katakana, Tamil, Bangla (Bengali) and Thai.

Regarding the observed drops in performance, only the one for the English to Korean Hangul task is significant. It is mainly due to the fact that the best performing system for this task in 2012 did not participate in the 2015 shared task.

6 Conclusions

The Shared Task on Machine Transliteration in NEWS 2015 has shown, once again, that the research community has a continued interest in this area. This report summarizes the results of the NEWS 2015 Shared Task.

We are pleased to report a comprehensive set of machine transliteration approaches and their evaluation results over two test sets: progress test (NEWS11) and evaluation test (NEWS12/15), as well as two conditions: standard runs and non-standard runs. While the standard runs allow for conducting meaningful comparisons across different algorithms, the non-standard runs open up more opportunities for exploiting a variety of additional linguistic resources.

Six teams from six different institutions participated in the shared task. In total, we received 97 standard and 6 non-standard runs for each test set; i.e. 194 standard and 12 non-standard runs in total. Most of the current state-of-the-art in machine transliteration is represented in the systems that have participated in the shared task.

Encouraged by the continued success of the NEWS workshop series, we plan to continue this event in the future to further promoting machine transliteration research and development.

Acknowledgments

The organizers of the NEWS 2015 Shared Task would like to thank the Institute for Infocomm Research (Singapore), Microsoft Research India, CJK Institute (Japan), National Electronics and Computer Technology Center (Thailand) and Sarvnaz Karim / RMIT for providing the corpora and technical support. Without those, the Shared Task would not be possible. We also want to thank all programme committee members for their valuable comments that improved the quality of the shared task papers. Finally, we wish to thank all participants for their active participation, which have made again the NEWS Machine Transliteration Shared Task a successful one.

References

Y. Al-Onaizan, K. Knight. 2002. Machine transliteration of names in arabic text. In Proc. ACL-2002Workshop: Computational Apporaches to Semitic Languages, Philadelphia, PA, USA.

D. Bahdanau, K. Cho, Y. Bengio. 2014. Neural machine translation by jointly learning to align and translate. Cornell University Library, arXiv:1409.0473 [cs.CL]

M. Bisani, H. Ney. 2008. Joint sequence models for grapheme-to-phoneme conversion. Speech Communication, 50(5):434–451.

CJKI. 2010. CJK Institute. http://www.cjk.org/.

D. Demner-Fushman, D.W. Oard. 2002. The effect of bilingual term list size on dictionary-based cross-language information retrieval. In Proc. 36-th Hawaii Int'l. Conf. System Sciences, volume 4, page 108.2.

A. Finch, P. Dixon, E. Sumita. 2012. Rescoring a phrase-based machine transliteration system with recurrent neural network language models. In Proceedings of the 4th Named Entity Workshop (NEWS) 2012, pages 47–51, Jeju, Korea, July.

A. Finch, L. Liu, X. Wang, E. Sumita. 2015. Neural Network Transduction Models in Transliteration Generation. In Proceedings of the 2015 Named Entities Workshop: Shared Task on Transliteration (NEWS 2015), Beijing, China.

W. Gao, K.F. Wong, W. Lam. 2004. Phoneme-based transliteration of foreign names for OOV problem. In Proc. IJCNLP, pages 374–381, Sanya, Hainan, China.

Y. Goldberg, M. Elhadad. 2008. Identification of transliterated foreign words in Hebrew script. In Proc. CICLing, volume LNCS 4919, pages 466–477.

D. Goldwasser, D. Roth. 2008. Transliteration as constrained optimization. In Proc. EMNLP, pages 353–362.

J. Halpern. 2007. The challenges and pitfalls of Arabic romanization and arabization. In Proc. Workshop on Comp. Approaches to Arabic Scriptbased Lang.

U. Hermjakob, K. Knight, H. Daum. 2008. Name translation in statistical machine translation: Learning when to transliterate. In Proc. ACL, Columbus, OH, USA, June.

S. Jiampojamarn, G. Kondrak, T. Sherif. 2007. Applying many-to-many alignments and hidden markov models to letter-to-phoneme conversion. In proceedings of Human Language Technologies 2007: The Conference of the North American Chapter of the Association for Computational Linguistics; pages 372–379, Rochester, New York, April.

S. Jiampojamarn, A. Bhargava, Q. Dou, K. Dwyer, G. Kondrak. 2009. DirecTL: a language independent approach to transliteration. In Proceedings of the 2009 Named Entities Workshop: Shared Task on Transliteration (NEWS 2009), pages 28–31, Suntec, Singapore.

S. Jiampojamarn, C. Cherry, G. Kondrak. 2010. Integrating joint n-gram features into a discriminative training framework. In Proceedings of NAACL-2010, Los Angeles, CA, June. Association for Computational Linguistics.

B.J. Kang, K.S. Choi. 2000. English-Korean automatic transliteration/ backtransliteration system and character alignment. In Proc. ACL, pages 17–18, Hong Kong.

A. Klementiev, D. Roth. 2006. Weakly supervised named entity transliteration and discovery from multilingual comparable corpora. In Proc. 21st Int'l Conf Computational Linguistics and 44th Annual Meeting of ACL, pages 817–824, Sydney, Australia, July.

K. Knight, J. Graehl. 1998. Machine transliteration. Computational Linguistics, 24(4).

P. Koehn, H. Hoang, A. Birch, C. Callison-Burch, M. Federico, N. Bertoldi, B. Cowan, W. Shen, C. Moran, R. Zens, C. Dyer, O. Bojar, A. Constantin, E. Herbst. 2007. Moses: Open source toolkit for statistical machine translation. In Proceedings of the 45th Annual Meeting of the Association for Computational Linguistics Companion Volume Proceedings of the Demo and Poster Sessions, pages 177–180, Prague, Czech Republic.

A. Kumaran, T. Kellner. 2007. A generic framework for machine transliteration. In Proc. SIGIR, pages 721–722.

A. Kunchukuttan, P. Bhattacharyya. 2015. Data representation methods and use of mined corpora for Indian language transliteration. In Proceedings of the 2015 Named Entities Workshop: Shared Task on Transliteration (NEWS 2015), Beijing, China.

H. Li, M. Zhang, J. Su. 2004. A joint source-channel model for machine transliteration. In Proc. 42nd ACL Annual Meeting, pages 159–166, Barcelona, Spain.

H. Li, A. Kumaran, V. Pervouchine, M. Zhang. 2009a. Report of NEWS 2009 machine transliteration shared task. In Proc. Named Entities Workshop at ACL 2009.

H. Li, A. Kumaran, M. Zhang, V. Pervouchine. 2009b. ACL-IJCNLP 2009 Named Entities Workshop - Shared Task on Transliteration. In Proc. Named Entities Workshop at ACL 2009.

H. Li, A. Kumaran, M. Zhang, V. Pervouchine. 2010a. Report of news 2010 transliteration generation shared task. In Proc. Named Entities Workshop at ACL 2010.

H. Li, A. Kumaran, M. Zhang, V. Pervouchine. 2010b. Whitepaper of news 2010 shared task on transliteration generation. In Proc. Named Entities Workshop at ACL 2010.

T. Mandl, C. Womser-Hacker. 2005. The effect of named entities on effectiveness in cross-language information retrieval evaluation. In Proc. ACM Symp. Applied Comp., pages 1059–1064.

H.M. Meng, W.K. Lo, B. Chen, K. Tang. 2001. Generate phonetic cognates to handle name entities in English-Chinese cross-language spoken document retrieval. In Proc. ASRU.

MSRI. 2009. Microsoft Research India. http://research.microsoft.com/india.

G. Nicolai, B. Hauer, M. Salameh, A. St Arnaud, Y. Xu, L. Yao, G. Kondrak. 2015. Multiple System Combination for Transliteration. In Proceedings of the 2015 Named Entities Workshop: Shared Task on Transliteration (NEWS 2015), Beijing, China.

J.H. Oh, K.S. Choi. 2002. An English-Korean transliteration model using pronunciation and contextual rules. In Proc. COLING 2002, Taipei, Taiwan.

Y. Shao, J. Tiedemann, J. Nivre. 2015. Boosting English-Chinese Machine Transliteration via High Quality Alignment and Multilingual Resources. In Proceedings of the 2015 Named Entities Workshop: Shared Task on Transliteration (NEWS 2015), Beijing, China.

T. Sherif, G. Kondrak. 2007. Substringbased transliteration. In Proc. 45th Annual Meeting of the ACL, pages 944–951, Prague, Czech Republic, June.

R. Sproat, T. Tao, C.X. Zhai. 2006. Named entity transliteration with comparable corpora. In Proc. 21st Int'l Conf Computational Linguistics and 44th Annual Meeting of ACL, pages 73–80, Sydney, Australia.

R. Udupa, K. Saravanan, A. Bakalov, A. Bhole. 2009. "They are out there, if you know where to look": Mining transliterations of OOV query terms for cross-language information retrieval. In LNCS: Advances in Information Retrieval, volume 5478, pages 437–448. Springer Berlin / Heidelberg.

P. Virga, S. Khudanpur. 2003. Transliteration of proper names in cross-lingual information retrieval. In Proc. ACL MLNER, Sapporo, Japan.

S. Wan, C.M. Verspoor. 1998. Automatic English-Chinese name transliteration for development of multilingual resources. In Proc. COLING, pages 1352–1356.

D. Wang, X. Yang, J. Xu, Y. Chen, N. Wang, B. Liu, J. Yang, Y. Zhang. 2015a. A Hybrid Transliteration Model for Chinese/English Named Entities — BJTU-NLP Report for the 5th Named Entities Workshop. In Proceedings of the 2015 Named Entities Workshop: Shared Task on Transliteration (NEWS 2015), Beijing, China.

Y.C. Wang, C.K. Wu, R.T.H. Tsai. 2015b. NCU IISR English-Korean and English-Chinese Named Entity Transliteration Using Different Grapheme Segmentation Approaches. In Proceedings of the 2015 Named Entities Workshop: Shared Task on Transliteration (NEWS 2015), Beijing, China.

D. Zelenko, C. Aone. 2006. Discriminative methods for transliteration. In Proc. EMNLP, pages 612–617, Sydney, Australia, July.

M. Zhang, A. Kumaran, H. Li. 2011a. Whitepaper of news 2011 shared task on machine transliteration. In Proc. Named Entities Workshop at IJCNLP 2011.

M. Zhang, H. Li, A. Kumaran, M. Liu. 2011b. Report of news 2011 machine transliteration shared task. In Proc. Named Entities Workshop at IJCNLP 2011.

M. Zhang, H. Li, A. Kumaran, M. Liu. 2012. Report of NEWS 2012 Machine Transliteration Shared Task. Proceedings of the 50th Annual Meeting of the Association for Computational Linguistics, pages 10–20, Jeju, Republic of Korea.

Appendix: Evaluation Results

Team	Submission	Test Set	ACC	F-score	MRR	MAP_{ref}
UPPS	***Run-1***	***NEWS11***	***0.333000***	***0.673433***	***0.387373***	***0.320348***
UPPS	Run-2	NEWS11	0.324000	0.681840	0.403869	0.311746
UPPS	Run-3	NEWS11	0.339500	0.694297	0.397274	0.326723
UPPS	Run-4	NEWS11	0.365000	0.708208	0.430950	0.351070
UPPS	Run-5	NEWS11	0.721500	0.869726	0.775266	0.717143
BJTU	***Run-1***	***NEWS11***	***0.223500***	***0.628967***	***0.223500***	***0.212291***
BJTU	Non-standard	NEWS11	0.224500	0.619581	0.224500	0.212253
NICT	***Run-1***	***NEWS11***	***0.344500***	***0.694670***	***0.448921***	***0.335733***
NICT	Run-2	NEWS11	0.213500	0.633107	0.250693	0.206071
IITB	***Run-1***	***NEWS11***	***0.303000***	***0.671143***	***0.391680***	***0.292121***
IITB	Run-2	NEWS11	0.177000	0.561347	0.212209	0.175762
NTU	***Run-1***	***NEWS11***	***0.232500***	***0.630283***	***0.232500***	***0.219895***
NTU	Run-2	NEWS11	0.292500	0.671896	0.292500	0.277193
UALB	***Run-1***	***NEWS11***	***0.331500***	***0.687510***	***0.413785***	***0.321167***

Table A1: Results for the English to Chinese transliteration task (EnCh) on Progress Test.

Team	Submission	Test Set	ACC	F-score	MRR	MAP_{ref}
UPPS	***Run-1***	***NEWS12/15***	***0.325397***	***0.660252***	***0.384383***	***0.313092***
UPPS	Run-2	NEWS12/15	0.310516	0.659662	0.396441	0.302924
UPPS	Run-3	NEWS12/15	0.335317	0.675918	0.396312	0.323261
UPPS	Run-4	NEWS12/15	0.373016	0.693169	0.436131	0.362703
UPPS	Run-5	NEWS12/15	0.655754	0.824023	0.735236	0.649278
BJTU	***Run-1***	***NEWS12/15***	***0.193452***	***0.605230***	***0.193452***	***0.182230***
BJTU	Non-standard	NEWS12/15	0.204365	0.604767	0.204365	0.195381
NICT	***Run-1***	***NEWS12/15***	***0.312500***	***0.665305***	***0.432201***	***0.305466***
NICT	Run-2	NEWS12/15	0.220238	0.627412	0.279823	0.216849
IITB	***Run-1***	***NEWS12/15***	***0.280754***	***0.638436***	***0.371490***	***0.273775***
IITB	Run-2	NEWS12/15	0.182540	0.545881	0.219496	0.180018
NTU	***Run-1***	***NEWS12/15***	***0.235119***	***0.623692***	***0.235119***	***0.224172***
NTU	Run-2	NEWS12/15	0.279762	0.645468	0.279762	0.265198
UALB	***Run-1***	***NEWS12/15***	***0.314484***	***0.663729***	***0.406026***	***0.305790***

Table A2: Results for the English to Chinese transliteration task (EnCh) on Evaluation Test.

Team	Submission	Test Set	ACC	F-score	MRR	MAP_{ref}
UPPS	***Run-1***	***NEWS11***	***0.150044***	***0.754860***	***0.228409***	***0.149603***
UPPS	Run-2	NEWS11	0.108561	0.731156	0.182593	0.108561
UPPS	Run-3	NEWS11	0.153133	0.768302	0.233491	0.152692
UPPS	Run-4	NEWS11	0.164607	0.772975	0.251579	0.164056
UPPS	Run-5	NEWS11	0.354369	0.833290	0.427793	0.353707
BJTU	***Run-1***	***NEWS11***	***0.105031***	***0.746174***	***0.105031***	***0.104700***
BJTU	Non-standard	NEWS11	0.151368	0.765544	0.151368	0.150927
NICT	***Run-1***	***NEWS11***	***0.158429***	***0.769593***	***0.252760***	***0.158760***
NICT	Run-2	NEWS11	0.115181	0.747071	0.176935	0.115512
IITB	***Run-1***	***NEWS11***	***0.105914***	***0.727373***	***0.176256***	***0.105914***
IITB	Run-2	NEWS11	0.048102	0.616609	0.083495	0.048102

Table A3: Results for the Chinese to English transliteration task (ChEn) on Progress Test.

Team	Submission	Test Set	ACC	F-score	MRR	MAP_{ref}
UPPS	***Run-1***	***NEWS12/15***	***0.191364***	***0.711462***	***0.271377***	***0.187057***
UPPS	Run-2	NEWS12/15	0.146222	0.712179	0.223034	0.143250
UPPS	Run-3	NEWS12/15	0.199215	0.752383	0.280989	0.194663
UPPS	Run-4	NEWS12/15	0.213935	0.745219	0.304566	0.212245
UPPS	Run-5	NEWS12/15	0.345437	0.805257	0.421142	0.345437
BJTU	***Run-1***	***NEWS12/15***	***0.157017***	***0.732100***	***0.157017***	***0.150720***
BJTU	Non-standard	NEWS12/15	0.157017	0.732100	0.157017	0.150720
NICT	***Run-1***	***NEWS12/15***	***0.184495***	***0.723785***	***0.283272***	***0.181196***
NICT	Run-2	NEWS12/15	0.136408	0.712954	0.205076	0.135509
IITB	***Run-1***	***NEWS12/15***	***0.141315***	***0.680611***	***0.214933***	***0.140361***
IITB	Run-2	NEWS12/15	0.077527	0.560009	0.107662	0.076927

Table A4: Results for the Chinese to English transliteration task (ChEn) on Evaluation Test.

Team	Submission	Test Set	ACC	F-score	MRR	MAP_{ref}
NICT	***Run-1***	***NEWS11***	***0.364532***	***0.679477***	***0.459777***	***0.361248***
NICT	Run-2	NEWS11	0.200328	0.588171	0.237128	0.196223
NTU	***Run-1***	***NEWS11***	***0.318555***	***0.657583***	***0.318555***	***0.311166***
NTU	Run-2	NEWS11	0.448276	0.725463	0.448276	0.439245
NTU	Run-3	NEWS11	0.274220	0.599985	0.274220	0.268883
NTU	Run-4	NEWS11	0.215107	0.570723	0.215107	0.209770
NTU	Run-5	NEWS11	0.042693	0.332851	0.042693	0.041461
NTU	Run-6	NEWS11	0.208539	0.527015	0.343186	0.204844
NTU	Run-7	NEWS11	0.499179	0.733029	0.539546	0.494253

Table A5: Results for the English to Korean Hangul transliteration task (EnKo) on Progress Test.

Team	Submission	Test Set	ACC	F-score	MRR	MAP_{ref}
NICT	***Run-1***	***NEWS12/15***	***0.363810***	***0.713655***	***0.447686***	***0.363333***
NICT	Run-2	NEWS12/15	0.188571	0.616223	0.231373	0.188095
NTU	***Run-1***	***NEWS12/15***	***0.327619***	***0.707843***	***0.327619***	***0.326905***
NTU	Run-2	NEWS12/15	0.445714	0.748241	0.445714	0.444762
NTU	Run-3	NEWS12/15	0.145714	0.522242	0.145714	0.145476
NTU	Run-4	NEWS12/15	0.174286	0.583525	0.174286	0.174048
NTU	Run-5	NEWS12/15	0.056190	0.375155	0.056190	0.056190
NTU	Run-6	NEWS12/15	0.195238	0.552238	0.334921	0.195000
NTU	Run-7	NEWS12/15	0.506667	0.761401	0.531746	0.505476

Table A6: Results for the English to Korean Hangul transliteration task (EnKo) on Evaluation Test.

Team	Submission	Test Set	ACC	F-score	MRR	MAP_{ref}
NICT	***Run-1***	***NEWS11***	***0.412121***	***0.807197***	***0.549902***	***0.411983***
NICT	Run-2	NEWS11	0.399449	0.796744	0.495723	0.399174
UALB	***Run-1***	***NEWS11***	***0.424793***	***0.806944***	***0.551851***	***0.424656***

Table A7: Results for the English to Japanese Katakana transliteration task (EnJa) on Progress Test.

Team	Submission	Test Set	ACC	F-score	MRR	MAP_{ref}
NICT	***Run-1***	***NEWS12/15***	***0.407551***	***0.815306***	***0.528128***	***0.404163***
NICT	Run-2	NEWS12/15	0.337851	0.784695	0.439676	0.337367
UALB	***Run-1***	***NEWS12/15***	***0.396902***	***0.811790***	***0.524526***	***0.394966***

Table A8:Results for the English to Japanese Katakana transliteration task (EnJa) on Evaluation Test.

Team	Submission	Test Set	ACC	F-score	MRR	MAP_{ref}
NICT	***Run-1***	***NEWS11***	***0.451839***	***0.637787***	***0.548539***	***0.451839***
NICT	Run-2	NEWS11	0.035026	0.320328	0.041669	0.035026

Table A9: Results for the English to Japanese Kanji transliteration task (JnJk) on Progress Test.

Team	Submission	Test Set	ACC	F-score	MRR	MAP_{ref}
NICT	***Run-1***	***NEWS12/15***	***0.534247***	***0.704960***	***0.610474***	***0.437821***
NICT	Run-2	NEWS12/15	0.031963	0.341456	0.042975	0.018189

Table A10: Results for the English to Japanese Kanji transliteration task (JnJk) on Evaluation Test.

Team	Submission	Test Set	ACC	F-score	MRR	MAP_{ref}
NICT	***Run-1***	***NEWS11***	***0.527048***	***0.927201***	***0.627657***	***0.390565***
NICT	Run-2	NEWS11	0.494204	0.891547	0.595463	0.370677
UALB	***Run-1***	***NEWS11***	***0.617079***	***0.941314***	***0.718896***	***0.435967***

Table A11: Results for the Arabic to English transliteration task (ArEn) on Progress Test.

Team	Submission	Test Set	ACC	F-score	MRR	MAP_{ref}
NICT	***Run-1***	***NEWS12/15***	***0.529412***	***0.928260***	***0.655920***	***0.459441***
NICT	Run-2	NEWS12/15	0.468858	0.914553	0.609188	0.405085
UALB	***Run-1***	***NEWS12/15***	***0.596021***	***0.935767***	***0.711291***	***0.477259***

Table A12: Results for the Arabic to English transliteration task (ArEn) on Evaluation Test.

Team	Submission	Test Set	ACC	F-score	MRR	MAP_{ref}
UALB	***Run-1***	***NEWS11***	***0.488000***	***0.883368***	***0.603763***	***0.486000***
UALB	Run-2	NEWS11	0.477000	0.881284	0.580941	0.475250
UALB	Non-standard	NEWS11	0.531000	0.901526	0.627492	0.530250
NICT	***Run-1***	***NEWS11***	***0.474000***	***0.881670***	***0.583569***	***0.472750***
NICT	Run-2	NEWS11	0.410000	0.855251	0.509001	0.409250
ITTB	***Run-1***	***NEWS11***	***0.434000***	***0.870109***	***0.556714***	***0.432750***
ITTB	Run-2	NEWS11	0.416000	0.860905	0.519782	0.413750
ITTB	Run-3	NEWS11	0.468000	0.873300	0.582212	0.465250
ITTB	Run-4	NEWS11	0.440000	0.867979	0.542456	0.439000
ITTB	Run-5	NEWS11	0.276000	0.814516	0.399723	0.275750
ITTB	Run-6	NEWS11	0.263000	0.806711	0.347494	0.263000

Table A13: Results for the English to Hindi transliteration task (EnHi) on Progress Test.

Team	Submission	Test Set	ACC	F-score	MRR	MAP_{ref}
UALB	***Run-1***	***NEWS12/15***	***0.649000***	***0.920225***	***0.730004***	***0.642778***
UALB	Run-2	NEWS12/15	0.558000	0.895520	0.657864	0.552889
UALB	Non-standard	NEWS12/15	0.559000	0.898486	0.661465	0.553750
NICT	***Run-1***	***NEWS12/15***	***0.696000***	***0.928536***	***0.753320***	***0.690167***
NICT	Run-2	NEWS12/15	0.641000	0.914722	0.702288	0.631861
ITTB	***Run-1***	***NEWS12/15***	***0.603000***	***0.907403***	***0.693690***	***0.598472***
ITTB	Run-2	NEWS12/15	0.584000	0.899290	0.671509	0.579417
ITTB	Run-3	NEWS12/15	0.621000	0.911463	0.710887	0.615083
ITTB	Run-4	NEWS12/15	0.599000	0.904661	0.686692	0.595639
ITTB	Run-5	NEWS12/15	0.303000	0.810614	0.411777	0.299222
ITTB	Run-6	NEWS12/15	0.295000	0.810716	0.382562	0.291972

Table A14: Results for the English to Hindi transliteration task (EnHi) on Evaluation Test.

Team	Submission	Test Set	ACC	F-score	MRR	MAP_{ref}
UALB	***Run-1***	***NEWS11***	***0.476000***	***0.907893***	***0.597020***	***0.474500***
UALB	Run-2	NEWS11	0.477000	0.906608	0.607133	0.476500
UALB	Non-standard	NEWS11	0.480000	0.907802	0.592867	0.479000
NICT	***Run-1***	***NEWS11***	***0.474000***	***0.904289***	***0.591604***	***0.471750***
NICT	Run-2	NEWS11	0.406000	0.879832	0.509260	0.403750
ITTB	***Run-1***	***NEWS11***	***0.383000***	***0.875980***	***0.524588***	***0.382500***
ITTB	Run-2	NEWS11	0.406000	0.887583	0.531215	0.405750
ITTB	Run-3	NEWS11	0.388000	0.875171	0.520549	0.386500
ITTB	Run-4	NEWS11	0.398000	0.883577	0.526356	0.398000
ITTB	Run-5	NEWS11	0.156000	0.774768	0.241502	0.156250
ITTB	Run-6	NEWS11	0.138000	0.770373	0.196521	0.138000

Table A15: Results for the English to Tamil transliteration task (EnTa) on Progress Test.

Team	Submission	Test Set	ACC	F-score	MRR	MAP_{ref}
UALB	***Run-1***	***NEWS12/15***	***0.537000***	***0.900219***	***0.633817***	***0.536500***
UALB	Run-2	NEWS12/15	0.585000	0.910232	0.679684	0.585000
UALB	Non-standard	NEWS12/15	0.528000	0.897556	0.620700	0.527250
NICT	***Run-1***	***NEWS12/15***	***0.626000***	***0.917861***	***0.702626***	***0.625000***
NICT	Run-2	NEWS12/15	0.584000	0.901983	0.649233	0.583500
ITTB	***Run-1***	***NEWS12/15***	***0.521000***	***0.894533***	***0.630000***	***0.521000***
ITTB	Run-2	NEWS12/15	0.542000	0.899063	0.640836	0.541750
ITTB	Run-3	NEWS12/15	0.520000	0.893332	0.626811	0.519750
ITTB	Run-4	NEWS12/15	0.543000	0.899800	0.643898	0.542750
ITTB	Run-5	NEWS12/15	0.142000	0.756809	0.228639	0.142250
ITTB	Run-6	NEWS12/15	0.139000	0.758239	0.190331	0.139250

Table A16: Results for the English to Tamil transliteration task (EnTa) on Evaluation Test.

Team	Submission	Test Set	ACC	F-score	MRR	MAP_{ref}
UALB	***Run-1***	***NEWS11***	***0.434000***	***0.883839***	***0.548446***	***0.433000***
UALB	Run-2	NEWS11	0.425000	0.885530	0.520380	0.423333
UALB	Non-standard	NEWS11	0.441000	0.893042	0.548766	0.439722
NICT	***Run-1***	***NEWS11***	***0.412000***	***0.877273***	***0.526961***	***0.410889***
NICT	Run-2	NEWS11	0.360000	0.858829	0.453091	0.358750
ITTB	***Run-1***	***NEWS11***	***0.373000***	***0.867258***	***0.489983***	***0.372722***
ITTB	Run-2	NEWS11	0.364000	0.864140	0.460513	0.362111

Table A17: Results for the English to Kannada transliteration task (EnKa) on Progress Test.

Team	Submission	Test Set	ACC	F-score	MRR	MAP_{ref}
UALB	***Run-1***	***NEWS12/15***	***0.545000***	***0.897336***	***0.643426***	***0.543861***
UALB	Run-2	NEWS12/15	0.475000	0.880163	0.582526	0.473861
UALB	Non-standard	NEWS12/15	0.491000	0.891682	0.600186	0.490361
NICT	***Run-1***	***NEWS12/15***	***0.562000***	***0.902859***	***0.647315***	***0.561361***
NICT	Run-2	NEWS12/15	0.546000	0.893315	0.611181	0.544611
ITTB	***Run-1***	***NEWS12/15***	***0.498000***	***0.882556***	***0.600849***	***0.497611***
ITTB	Run-2	NEWS12/15	0.505000	0.882445	0.590167	0.504361

Table A18: Results for the English to Kannada transliteration task (EnKa) on Evaluation Test.

Team	Submission	Test Set	ACC	F-score	MRR	MAP_{ref}
NICT	***Run-1***	***NEWS11***	***0.479000***	***0.891883***	***0.592440***	***0.477000***
NICT	Run-2	NEWS11	0.375000	0.852264	0.467951	0.373250
ITTB	***Run-1***	***NEWS11***	***0.470000***	***0.887156***	***0.584836***	***0.467750***
ITTB	Run-2	NEWS11	0.442000	0.881586	0.547812	0.441500
ITTB	Run-3	NEWS11	0.453000	0.876508	0.571826	0.452000
ITTB	Run-4	NEWS11	0.435000	0.880181	0.543165	0.434750
ITTB	Run-5	NEWS11	0.234000	0.799288	0.338209	0.233750
ITTB	Run-6	NEWS11	0.241000	0.809643	0.309816	0.240500
UALB	***Run-1***	***NEWS11***	***0.509000***	***0.897792***	***0.619730***	***0.507500***

Table A19: Results for the English to Bangla (Bengali) transliteration task (EnBa) on Progress Test.

Team	Submission	Test Set	ACC	F-score	MRR	MAP_{ref}
NICT	***Run-1***	***NEWS12/15***	***0.483000***	***0.897317***	***0.590843***	***0.482667***
NICT	Run-2	NEWS12/15	0.364000	0.847578	0.465787	0.361750
ITTB	***Run-1***	***NEWS12/15***	***0.441000***	***0.885009***	***0.567487***	***0.439917***
ITTB	Run-2	NEWS12/15	0.422000	0.876431	0.530971	0.420417
ITTB	Run-3	NEWS12/15	0.451000	0.882013	0.575119	0.449667
ITTB	Run-4	NEWS12/15	0.432000	0.875988	0.541814	0.430528
ITTB	Run-5	NEWS12/15	0.238000	0.796878	0.342817	0.238000
ITTB	Run-6	NEWS12/15	0.238000	0.806505	0.320520	0.235778
UALB	***Run-1***	***NEWS12/15***	***0.492000***	***0.897661***	***0.608379***	***0.491028***

Table A20: Results for the English to Bangla (Bengali) transliteration task (EnBa) on Evaluation Test.

Team	Submission	Test Set	ACC	F-score	MRR	MAP_{ref}
UALB	***Run-1***	***NEWS11***	***0.622000***	***0.933084***	***0.725101***	***0.622000***
UALB	Run-2	NEWS11	0.622000	0.936077	0.733577	0.622000
UALB	Non-standard	NEWS11	0.616000	0.934090	0.722406	0.616000
NICT	***Run-1***	***NEWS11***	***0.609000***	***0.933595***	***0.715783***	***0.609000***
NICT	Run-2	NEWS11	0.558000	0.918467	0.646346	0.558000
ITTB	***Run-1***	***NEWS11***	***0.041000***	***0.739161***	***0.059080***	***0.041000***
ITTB	Run-2	NEWS11	0.000000	0.008072	0.000000	0.000000

Table A21: Results for the English to Hebrew transliteration task (EnHe) on Progress Test.

Team	Submission	Test Set	ACC	F-score	MRR	MAP_{ref}
UALB	***Run-1***	***NEWS12/15***	***0.173636***	***0.803924***	***0.252981***	***0.172273***
UALB	Run-2	NEWS12/15	0.180000	0.805826	0.271303	0.179318
UALB	Non-standard	NEWS12/15	0.183636	0.805540	0.257166	0.181818
NICT	***Run-1***	***NEWS12/15***	***0.179091***	***0.807675***	***0.257256***	***0.178636***
NICT	Run-2	NEWS12/15	0.162727	0.796318	0.217959	0.160909
ITTB	***Run-1***	***NEWS12/15***	***0.008182***	***0.699630***	***0.016538***	***0.008182***
ITTB	Run-2	NEWS12/15	0.000000	0.006314	0.000000	0.000000

Table A22: Results for the English to Hebrew transliteration task (EnHe) on Evaluation Test.

Team	Submission	Test Set	ACC	F-score	MRR	MAP_{ref}
NICT	***Run-1***	***NEWS11***	***0.387000***	***0.866853***	***0.488948***	***0.383153***
NICT	Run-2	NEWS11	0.358500	0.800512	0.443323	0.354538
ITTB	***Run-1***	***NEWS11***	***0.312000***	***0.841161***	***0.425847***	***0.310233***
ITTB	Run-2	NEWS11	0.284500	0.837963	0.384735	0.281712
UALB	***Run-1***	***NEWS11***	***0.410000***	***0.871492***	***0.519079***	***0.404424***

Table A23: Results for the English to Thai transliteration task (EnTh) on Progress Test.

Team	Submission	Test Set	ACC	F-score	MRR	MAP_{ref}
NICT	***Run-1***	***NEWS12/15***	***0.156958***	***0.757421***	***0.213140***	***0.156958***
NICT	Run-2	NEWS12/15	0.131877	0.742635	0.195015	0.131877
ITTB	***Run-1***	***NEWS12/15***	***0.118932***	***0.735916***	***0.185874***	***0.118932***
ITTB	Run-2	NEWS12/15	0.102751	0.733311	0.149795	0.102751
UALB	***Run-1***	***NEWS12/15***	***0.140777***	***0.751829***	***0.208695***	***0.140777***

Table A24: Results for the English to Thai transliteration task (EnTh) on Evaluation Test.

Team	Submission	Test Set	ACC	F-score	MRR	MAP_{ref}
NICT	***Run-1***	***NEWS11***	***0.276923***	***0.846328***	***0.425615***	***0.278711***
NICT	Run-2	NEWS11	0.178462	0.807659	0.302689	0.180481
ITTB	***Run-1***	***NEWS11***	***0.247692***	***0.830477***	***0.402999***	***0.250661***
ITTB	Run-2	NEWS11	0.247692	0.833104	0.376071	0.248732
UALB	***Run-1***	***NEWS11***	***0.272821***	***0.845536***	***0.432649***	***0.274439***

Table A25: Results for the Thai to English transliteration task (ThEn) on Progress Test.

Team	Submission	Test Set	ACC	F-score	MRR	MAP_{ref}
NICT	***Run-1***	***NEWS12/15***	***0.153722***	***0.781110***	***0.226355***	***0.153722***
NICT	Run-2	NEWS12/15	0.129450	0.762891	0.189012	0.129450
ITTB	***Run-1***	***NEWS12/15***	***0.115696***	***0.757194***	***0.197850***	***0.115696***
ITTB	Run-2	NEWS12/15	0.101133	0.746325	0.161466	0.101133
UALB	***Run-1***	***NEWS12/15***	***0.156149***	***0.774646***	***0.241982***	***0.156149***

Table A26: Results for the Thai to English transliteration task (ThEn) on Evaluation Test.

Team	Submission	Test Set	ACC	F-score	MRR	MAP_{ref}
UALB	***Run-1***	***NEWS11***	***0.381500***	***0.860210***	***0.517000***	***0.375188***
UALB	Run-2	NEWS11	0.360500	0.853419	0.476237	0.354408
NICT	***Run-1***	***NEWS11***	***0.359500***	***0.852437***	***0.471200***	***0.354309***
NICT	Run-2	NEWS11	0.329000	0.837196	0.425778	0.324021
ITTB	***Run-1***	***NEWS11***	***0.342000***	***0.844966***	***0.468104***	***0.336937***
ITTB	Run-2	NEWS11	0.335000	0.847316	0.453176	0.333686

Table A27: Results for the English to Persian transliteration task (EnPe) on Progress Test.

Team	Submission	Test Set	ACC	F-score	MRR	MAP_{ref}
UALB	***Run-1***	***NEWS12/15***	***0.683301***	***0.942521***	***0.782315***	***0.658255***
UALB	Run-2	NEWS12/15	0.710173	0.949957	0.807624	0.690791
NICT	***Run-1***	***NEWS12/15***	***0.696737***	***0.948468***	***0.789989***	***0.682543***
NICT	Run-2	NEWS12/15	0.565259	0.911092	0.668964	0.550183
ITTB	***Run-1***	***NEWS12/15***	***0.619962***	***0.929311***	***0.740966***	***0.604472***
ITTB	Run-2	NEWS12/15	0.622841	0.931697	0.723980	0.610456

Table A28: Results for the English to Persian transliteration task (EnPe) on Evaluation Test.

Keynote Speech: How do you spell that? A journey through word representations

Greg Kondrak
Department of Computing Science
University of Alberta
gkondrak@ualberta.ca

Abstract

Languages are made up of words, which in turn consist of smaller units such as letters, phonemes, morphemes and syllables. Words exist independently of writing, as abstract entities shared among the speakers of a language. Those abstract entities have various representations, which in turn may have different realizations. Orthographic forms, phonetic transcriptions, alternative transliterations, and even sound-wave spectrograms are all related by referring to the same abstract word and they all convey information about its pronunciation. In this talk, I will discuss the lessons learned and insights gained from a number of research projects related to the transliteration task in which I participated.

Bio.

Greg Kondrak is an Associate Professor at the Department of Computing Science, University of Alberta. He has served four times as an Area Chair for the ACL conference. He is currently the Secretary of the Special Interest Group on Computational Morphology and Phonology (SIGMORPHON). His research is focused on natural language processing at the sub-word level, including transliteration, grapheme-to-phoneme conversion, and phonetic similarity. Since 2007, he has co-authored five conference papers devoted to transliteration, and participated in all five editions of the NEWS shared task on transliteration. Altogether, he has published over 70 papers, most of which can be found in the ACL Anthology.

Proceedings of the Fifth Named Entity Workshop, joint with 53rd ACL and the 7th IJCNLP, page 24,
Beijing, China, July 26-31, 2015. ©2015 Association for Computational Linguistics

Boosting Named Entity Recognition with Neural Character Embeddings

Cícero dos Santos
IBM Research
138/146 Av. Pasteur
Rio de Janeiro, RJ, Brazil
cicerons@br.ibm.com

Victor Guimarães
Instituto de Computação
Universidade Federal Fluminense (UFF)
Niterói, RJ, Rio de Janeiro
victorguimaraes@id.uff.br

Abstract

Most state-of-the-art named entity recognition (NER) systems rely on handcrafted features and on the output of other NLP tasks such as part-of-speech (POS) tagging and text chunking. In this work we propose a language-independent NER system that uses automatically learned features only. Our approach is based on the CharWNN deep neural network, which uses word-level and character-level representations (embeddings) to perform sequential classification. We perform an extensive number of experiments using two annotated corpora in two different languages: HAREM I corpus, which contains texts in Portuguese; and the SPA CoNLL-2002 corpus, which contains texts in Spanish. Our experimental results give evidence of the contribution of neural character embeddings for NER. Moreover, we demonstrate that the same neural network which has been successfully applied to POS tagging can also achieve state-of-the-art results for language-independet NER, using the same hyperparameters, and without any handcrafted features. For the HAREM I corpus, CharWNN outperforms the state-of-the-art system by 7.9 points in the F1-score for the total scenario (ten NE classes). For the SPA CoNLL-2002 corpus, CharWNN outperforms the state-of-the-art system by 0.8 point in the F1.

1 Introduction

Named entity recognition is a natural language processing (NLP) task that consists of finding names in a text and classifying them among several predefined categories of interest such as person, organization, location and time. Although machine learning based systems have been the predominant approach to achieve state-of-the-art results for NER, most of these NER systems rely on the use of costly handcrafted features and on the output of other NLP tasks (Tjong Kim Sang, 2002; Tjong Kim Sang and De Meulder, 2003; Doddington et al., 2004; Finkel et al., 2005; Milidiú et al., 2007). On the other hand, some recent work on NER have used deep learning strategies which minimize the need of these costly features (Chen et al., 2010; Collobert et al., 2011; Passos et al., 2014; Tang et al., 2014). However, as far as we know, there are still no work on deep learning approaches for NER that use character-level embeddings.

In this paper we approach language-independent NER using CharWNN, a recently proposed deep neural network (DNN) architecture that jointly uses word-level and character-level embeddings to perform sequential classification (dos Santos and Zadrozny, 2014a). CharWNN employs a convolutional layer that allows effective character-level feature extraction from words of any size. This approach has proven to be very effective for language-independent POS tagging (dos Santos and Zadrozny, 2014a; dos Santos and Zadrozny, 2014b).

We perform an extensive number of experiments using two annotated corpora: HAREM I corpus, which contains texts in Portuguese; and the SPA CoNLL-2002, which contains texts in Spanish. In our experiments, we compare the performance of the joint and individual use of character-level and word-level embeddings. We provide information on the impact of unsupervised pre-training of word embeddings in the performance of our proposed NER approach. Our experimental results evidence that CharWNN is effective and robust for Portuguese and Spanish NER. Using the same CharWNN configuration used by dos Santos and Zadrozny (2014) for POS Tagging,

Proceedings of the Fifth Named Entity Workshop, joint with 53rd ACL and the 7th IJCNLP, pages 25–33,
Beijing, China, July 26-31, 2015. ©2015 Association for Computational Linguistics

we achieve state-of-the-art results for both corpora. For the HAREM I corpus, CharWNN outperforms the state-of-the-art system by 7.9 points in the F1-score for the *total scenario* (ten NE classes), and by 7.2 points in the F1 for the *selective scenario* (five NE classes). For the SPA CoNLL-2002 corpus, CharWNN outperforms the state-of-the-art system by 0.8 point in the F1.

This work is organized as follows. In Section 2, we briefly describe the CharWNN architecture. Section 3 details our experimental setup and Section 4 discuss our experimental results. Section 6 presents our final remarks.

2 CharWNN

CharWNN extends Collobert et al.'s (2011) neural network architecture for sequential classification by adding a convolutional layer to extract character-level representations (dos Santos and Zadrozny, 2014a). Given a sentence, the network gives for each word a score for each class (tag) $\tau \in T$. As depicted in Figure 1, in order to score a word, the network takes as input a fixed-sized window of words centred around the target word. The input is passed through a sequence of layers where features with increasing levels of complexity are extracted. The output for the whole sentence is then processed using the Viterbi algorithm (Viterbi, 1967) to perform structured prediction. For a detailed description of the CharWNN neural network we refer the reader to (dos Santos and Zadrozny, 2014a).

2.1 Word- and Character-level Embeddings

As illustrated in Figure 1, the first layer of the network transforms words into real-valued feature vectors (embeddings). These embeddings are meant to capture morphological, syntactic and semantic information about the words. We use a fixed-sized word vocabulary V^{wrd}, and we consider that words are composed of characters from a fixed-sized character vocabulary V^{chr}. Given a sentence consisting of N words $\{w_1, w_2, ..., w_N\}$, every word w_n is converted into a vector $u_n = [r^{wrd}; r^{wch}]$, which is composed of two subvectors: the *word-level embedding* $r^{wrd} \in \mathbb{R}^{d^{wrd}}$ and the *character-level embedding* $r^{wch} \in \mathbb{R}^{cl_u}$ of w_n. While word-level embeddings capture syntactic and semantic information, character-level embeddings capture morphological and shape information.

Word-level embeddings are encoded by column vectors in an embedding matrix $W^{wrd} \in \mathbb{R}^{d^{wrd} \times |V^{wrd}|}$, and retrieving the embedding of a particular word consists in a simple matrix-vector multiplication. The matrix W^{wrd} is a parameter to be learned, and the size of the word-level embedding d^{wrd} is a hyperparameter to be set by the user.

The *character-level embedding* of each word is computed using a convolutional layer (Waibel et al., 1989; Lecun et al., 1998). In Figure 1, we illustrate the construction of the character-level embedding for the word *Bennett*, but the same process is used to construct the character-level embedding of each word in the input. The convolutional layer first produces local features around each character of the word, and then combines them using a max operation to create a fixed-sized character-level embedding of the word.

Given a word w composed of M characters $\{c_1, c_2, ..., c_M\}$, we first transform each character c_m into a character embedding r^{chr}_m. Character embeddings are encoded by column vectors in the embedding matrix $W^{chr} \in \mathbb{R}^{d^{chr} \times |V^{chr}|}$. Given a character c, its embedding r^{chr} is obtained by the matrix-vector product: $r^{chr} = W^{chr} v^c$, where v^c is a vector of size $\left|V^{chr}\right|$ which has value 1 at index c and zero in all other positions. The input for the convolutional layer is the sequence of character embeddings $\{r^{chr}_1, r^{chr}_2, ..., r^{chr}_M\}$.

The convolutional layer applies a matrix-vector operation to each window of size k^{chr} of successive windows in the sequence $\{r^{chr}_1, r^{chr}_2, ..., r^{chr}_M\}$. Let us define the vector $z_m \in \mathbb{R}^{d^{chr}k^{chr}}$ as the concatenation of the character embedding m, its $(k^{chr} - 1)/2$ left neighbors, and its $(k^{chr} - 1)/2$ right neighbors:

$$z_m = \left(r^{chr}_{m-(k^{chr}-1)/2}, ..., r^{chr}_{m+(k^{chr}-1)/2}\right)^T$$

The convolutional layer computes the j-th element of the vector r^{wch}, which is the character-level embedding of w, as follows:

$$[r^{wch}]_j = \max_{1<m<M} \left[W^0 z_m + b^0\right]_j \quad (1)$$

where $W^0 \in \mathbb{R}^{cl_u \times d^{chr}k^{chr}}$ is the weight matrix of the convolutional layer. The same matrix is used to extract local features around each character window of the given word. Using the max over all character windows of the word, we extract a fixed-sized feature vector for the word.

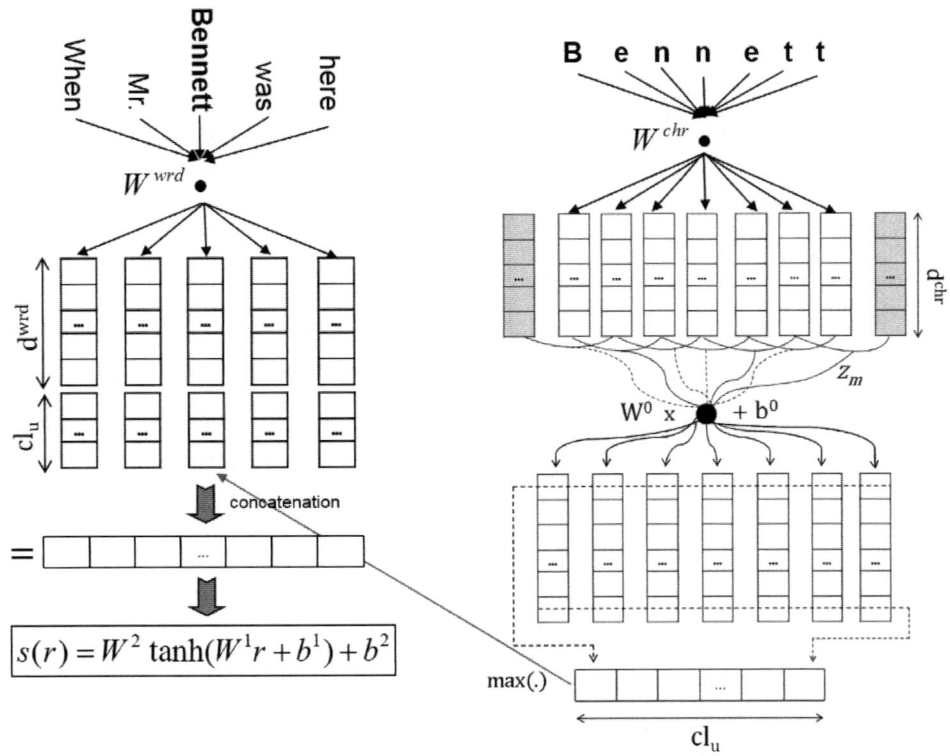

Figure 1: CharWNN Architecture

Matrices W^{chr} and W^0, and vector b^0 are parameters to be learned. The size of the character vector d^{chr}, the number of convolutional units cl_u (which corresponds to the size of the character-level embedding of a word), and the size of the character context window k^{chr} are hyperparameters.

2.2 Scoring and Structured Inference

We follow Collobert et al.'s (Collobert et al., 2011) window approach to score all tags T for each word in a sentence. This approach follows the assumption that in sequential classification the tag of a word depends mainly on its neighboring words. Given a sentence with N words $\{w_1, w_2, ..., w_N\}$, which have been converted to joint word-level and character-level embedding $\{u_1, u_2, ..., u_N\}$, to compute tag scores for the n-th word w_n in the sentence, we first create a vector r resulting from the concatenation of a sequence of k^{wrd} embeddings, centralized in the n-th word:

$$r = \left(u_{n-(k^{wrd}-1)/2}, ..., u_{n+(k^{wrd}-1)/2}\right)^T$$

We use a special *padding token* for the words with indices outside of the sentence boundaries.

Next, the vector r is processed by two usual neural network layers, which extract one more level of representation and compute the scores:

$$s(w_n) = W^2 h(W^1 r + b^1) + b^2 \qquad (2)$$

where matrices $W^1 \in \mathbb{R}^{hl_u \times k^{wrd}(d^{wrd}+cl_u)}$ and $W^2 \in \mathbb{R}^{|T| \times hl_u}$, and vectors $b^1 \in \mathbb{R}^{hl_u}$ and $b^2 \in \mathbb{R}^{|T|}$ are parameters to be learned. The transfer function $h(.)$ is the hyperbolic tangent. The size of the context window k^{wrd} and the number of hidden units hl_u are hyperparameters to be chosen by the user.

Like in (Collobert et al., 2011), CharWNN uses a prediction scheme that takes into account the sentence structure. The method uses a transition score A_{tu} for jumping from tag $t \in T$ to $u \in T$ in successive words, and a score A_{0t} for starting from the t-th tag. Given the sentence $[w]_1^N = \{w_1, w_2, ..., w_N\}$, the score for tag path

$[t]_1^N = \{t_1, t_2, ..., t_N\}$ is computed as follows:

$$S\left([w]_1^N, [t]_1^N, \theta\right) = \sum_{n=1}^{N} \left(A_{t_{n-1}t_n} + s(w_n)_{t_n}\right) \tag{3}$$

where $s(w_n)_{t_n}$ is the score given for tag t_n at word w_n and θ is the set of all trainable network parameters $\left(W^{wrd}, W^{chr}, W^0, b^0, W^1, b^1, W^2, b^2, A\right)$.

After scoring each word in the sentence, the Viterbi algorithm (Viterbi, 1967) is used to find the most likely tag sequence $[t^*]_1^N$, which consists in the tag path that leads to the maximal score:

$$[t^*]_1^N =_{[t]_1^N \in T^N} S\left([w]_1^N, [t]_1^N, \theta\right) \tag{4}$$

2.3 Network Training

We train CharWNN by minimizing a negative likelihood over the training set D. In the same way as in (Collobert et al., 2011), we interpret the sentence score (3) as a conditional probability over a path. For this purpose, we exponentiate the score (3) and normalize it with respect to all possible paths. Taking the log, we arrive at the following conditional log-probability:

$$\log p\left([t]_1^N | [w]_1^N, \theta\right) = S\left([w]_1^N, [t]_1^N, \theta\right) - \log\left(\sum_{\forall [u]_1^N \in T^N} e^{S\left([w]_1^N, [u]_1^N, \theta\right)}\right) \tag{5}$$

The log-likelihood in Equation 5 can be computed efficiently using dynamic programming (Collobert, 2011). We use stochastic gradient descent (SGD) to minimize the negative log-likelihood with respect to θ. We use the backpropagation algorithm to compute the gradients of the neural network. We implemented CharWNN using the *Theano* library (Bergstra et al., 2010).

3 Experimental Setup

3.1 Unsupervised Learning of Word Embeddings

The word embeddings used in our experiments are initialized by means of unsupervised pre-training. We perform pre-training of word-level embeddings using the skip-gram NN architecture (Mikolov et al., 2013) available in the word2vec [1] tool.

In our experiments on Portuguese NER, we use the word-level embeddings previously trained by dos Santos and Zadrozny (2014a). They have used a corpus composed of the Portuguese Wikipedia, the CETENFolha[2] corpus and the CETEMPublico[3] corpus.

In our experiments on Spanish NER, we use the Spanish Wikipedia. We process the Spanish Wikipedia corpus using the same steps used by dos Santos and Zadrozny (2014a): (1) remove paragraphs that are not in Spanish; (2) substitute non-roman characters by a special character; (3) tokenize the text using a tokenizer that we have implemented; (4) remove sentences that are less than 20 characters long (including white spaces) or have less than 5 tokens; (5) lowercase all words and substitute each numerical digit by a 0. The resulting corpus contains around 450 million tokens.

It is important to note that although we perform unsupervised pre-training of word embeddings, we also leave the word embeddings be updated during the supervised step, i.e., during the training with the NER labeled data.

Following dos Santos and Zadrozny (2014a), we do not perform unsupervised learning of character-level embeddings. The character-level embeddings are initialized by randomly sampling each value from an uniform distribution: $\mathcal{U}(-r, r)$, where $r = \sqrt{\frac{6}{|V^{chr}| + d^{chr}}}$. The weight matrices W^0, W^1 and W^2 are initialized in a similar way.

3.2 Corpora

We use the corpus from the first HAREM evaluation (Santos and Cardoso, 2007) in our experiments on Portuguese NER. This corpus is annotated with ten named entity categories: Person (PESSOA), Organization (ORGANIZACAO), Location (LOCAL), Value (VALOR), Date (TEMPO), Abstraction (ABSTRACCAO), Title (OBRA), Event (ACONTECIMENTO), Thing (COISA) and Other (OUTRO). The HAREM corpus is already divided into two subsets: First HAREM and MiniHAREM. Each subset corresponds to a different Portuguese NER contest. In our experiments, we call HAREM I the setup where we use the First HAREM corpus as the training set and the MiniHAREM corpus as the test set. This is the same setup used by dos Santos and Milidiú (2012). Additionally, we tokenize the

[1] http://code.google.com/p/word2vec/

[2] http://www.linguateca.pt/cetenfolha/

[3] http://www.linguateca.pt/cetempublico/

Table 1: Named Entity Recognition Corpora.

Corpus	Language	Training Data		Test Data	
		Sentenc.	Tokens	Sentenc.	Tokens
HAREM I	Portuguese	4,749	93,125	3,393	62,914
SPA CoNLL-2002	Spanish	8,323	264,715	1,517	51,533

HAREM corpus and create a development set that comprises 5% of the training set. Table 1 present some details of this dataset.

In our experiments on Spanish NER we use the SPA CoNLL-2002 Corpus, which was developed for the CoNLL-2002 shared task (Tjong Kim Sang, 2002). It is annotated with four named entity categories: Person, Organization, Location and Miscellaneous. The SPA CoNLL-2002 corpus is already divided into training, development and test sets. The development set has characteristics similar to the test corpora.

We treat NER as a sequential classification problem. Hence, in both corpora we use the *IOB2* tagging style where: *O*, means that the word is not a NE; *B-X* is used for the leftmost word of a NE type *X*; and *I-X* means that the word is inside of a NE type *X*. The *IOB2* tagging style is illustrated in the following example.

```
Wolff/B-PER ,/O currently/O a/O
journalist/O in/O Argentina/B-LOC ,/O
played/O with/O Del/B-PER Bosque/I-PER
in/O the/O final/O years/O of/O the/O
seventies/O in/O Real/B-ORG
Madrid/I-ORG
```

3.3 Model Setup

In most of our experiments, we use the same hyperparameters used by dos Santos and Zadrozny (2014) for part-of-speech tagging. The only exception is the learning rate for SPA CoNLL-2002, which we set to 0.005 in order to avoid divergence. The hyperparameter values are presented in Table 2. We use the development sets to determine the number of training epochs, which is six for HAREM and sixteen for SPA CoNLL-2002.

We compare CharWNN with two similar neural network architectures: CharNN and WNN. CharNN is equivalent to CharWNN without word embeddings, i.e., it uses character-level embeddings only. WNN is equivalent to CharWNN without character-level embeddings, i.e., it uses word embeddings only. Additionally, in the same way as in (Collobert et al., 2011), we check the impact of adding to WNN two handcrafted features that contain character-level information, namely capitalization and suffix. The capitalization feature has five possible values: all lowercased, first uppercased, all uppercased, contains an uppercased letter, and all other cases. We use suffix of size three. In our experiments, both capitalization and suffix embeddings have dimension five. The hyperparameters values for these two NNs are shown in Table 2.

4 Experimental Results

4.1 Results for Spanish NER

In Table 3, we report the performance of different NNs for the SPA CoNLL-2002 corpus. All results for this corpus were computed using the CoNLL-2002 evaluation script[4]. CharWNN achieves the best precision, recall and F1 in both development and test sets. For the test set, the F1 of CharWNN is 3 points larger than the F1 of the WNN that uses two additional handcrafted features: suffixes and capitalization. This result suggests that, for the NER task, the character-level embeddings are as or more effective as the two character-level features used in WNN. Similar results were obtained by dos Santos and Zadrozny (2014) in the POS tagging task.

In the two last lines of Table 3 we can see the results of using word embeddings and character-level embeddings separately. Both, WNN that uses word embeddings only and CharNN, do not achieve results competitive with the results of the networks that jointly use word-level and character-level information. This is not surprising, since it is already known in the NLP community that jointly using word-level and character-level features is important to perform named entity recognition.

In Table 4, we compare CharWNN results with the ones of a state-of-the-art system for the SPA CoNLL-2002 Corpus. This system was trained using AdaBoost and is described in (Carreras et al., 2002). It employs decision trees as a base learner

[4]http://www.cnts.ua.ac.be/conll2002/ner/bin/conlleval.txt

Table 2: Neural Network Hyperparameters.

Parameter	Parameter Name	CharWNN	WNN	CharNN
d^{wrd}	Word embedding dimensions	100	100	-
k^{wrd}	Word context window size	5	5	5
d^{chr}	Char. embedding dimensions	10	-	50
k^{chr}	Char. context window size	5	-	5
cl_u	Convolutional units	50	-	200
hl_u	Hidden units	300	300	300
λ	Learning rate	0.0075	0.0075	0.0075

Table 3: Comparison of different NNs for the SPA CoNLL-2002 corpus.

NN	Features	Dev. Set			Test Set		
		Prec.	Rec.	F1	Prec.	Rec.	F1
CharWNN	word emb., char emb.	**80.13**	**78.68**	**79.40**	**82.21**	**82.21**	**82.21**
WNN	word emb., suffix, capit.	78.33	76.31	77.30	79.64	78.67	79.15
WNN	word embeddings	73.87	68.45	71.06	73.77	68.19	70.87
CharNN	char embeddings	53.86	51.40	52.60	61.13	59.03	60.06

and uses handcrafted features as input. Among others, these features include gazetteers with people names and geographical location names. The AdaBoost based system divide the NER task into two intermediate sub-tasks: NE identification and NE classification. In the first sub-task, the system identifies NE candidates. In the second sub-task, the system classifies the identified candidates. In Table 4, we can see that even using only automatically learned features, CharWNN achieves state-of-the-art results for the SPA CoNLL-2002.

4.2 Results for Portuguese NER

In Table 5, we report the performance of different NNs for the HAREM I corpus. The results in this table were computed using the CoNLL-2002 evaluation script. We report results in two scenarios: total and selective. In the *total* scenario, all ten categories are taken into account when scoring the systems. In the *selective* scenario, only five chosen categories (Person, Organization, Location, Date and Value) are taken into account. We can see in Table 5, that CharWNN and WNN that uses two additional handcrafted features have similar results. We think that by increasing the training data, CharWNN has the potential to learn better character embeddings and outperform WNN, like happens in the SPA CoNLL-2002 corpus, which is larger than the HAREM I corpus. Again, CharNN and WNN that uses word embeddings only, do not achieve results competitive with the results of the networks that jointly use word-level and character-level information.

In order to compare CharWNN results with the one of the state-of-the-art system, we report in tables 6 and 7 the precision, recall, and F1 scores computed with the evaluation scripts from the HAREM I competition[5] (Santos and Cardoso, 2007), which uses a scoring strategy different from the CoNLL-2002 evaluation script.

In Table 6, we compare CharWNN results with the ones of ETL_{CMT}, a state-of-the-art system for the HAREM I Corpus (dos Santos and Milidiú, 2012). ETL_{CMT} is an ensemble method that uses Entropy Guided Transformation Learning (ETL) as the base learner. The ETL_{CMT} system uses handcrafted features like gazetteers and dictionaries as well as the output of other NLP tasks such as POS tagging and noun phrase (NP) chunking. As we can see in Table 6, CharWNN outperforms the state-of-the-art system by a large margin in both total and selective scenarios.

In Table 7, we compare CharWNN results by entity type with the ones of ETL_{CMT}. These results were computed in the selective scenario. CharWNN produces a much better recall than ETL_{CMT} for the classes LOC, PER and ORG. For the ORG entity, the improvement is of 21 points in the recall. We believe that a large part of this boost in the recall is due to the unsupervised pre-

[5] http://www.linguateca.pt/primeiroHAREM/harem_Arquitectura.html

Table 4: Comparison with the state-of-the-art for the SPA CoNLL-2002 corpus.

System	Features	Prec.	Rec.	F1
CharWNN	word embeddings, char embeddings	**82.21**	**82.21**	**82.21**
AdaBoost	words, ortographic, POS tags, trigger words, bag-of-words, gazetteers, word suffixes, word type patterns, entity length	81.38	81.40	81.39

Table 5: Comparison of different NNs for the HAREM I corpus.

NN	Features	Total Scenario			Selective Scenario		
		Prec.	Rec.	F1	Prec.	Rec.	F1
CharWNN	word emb., char emb.	67.16	**63.74**	65.41	73.98	**68.68**	71.23
WNN	word emb., suffix, capit.	**68.52**	63.16	**65.73**	**75.05**	68.35	**71.54**
WNN	word embeddings	63.32	53.23	57.84	68.91	58.77	63.44
CharNN	char embeddings	57.10	50.65	53.68	66.30	54.54	59.85

Table 6: Comparison with the State-of-the-art for the HAREM I corpus.

System	Features	Total Scenario			Selective Scenario		
		Prec.	Rec.	F1	Prec.	Rec.	F1
CharWNN	word emb., char emb.	74.54	**68.53**	**71.41**	**78.38**	**77.49**	**77.93**
ETL_{CMT}	words, POS tags, NP tags, capitalization, word length, dictionaries, gazetteers	**77.52**	53.86	63.56	77.27	65.20	70.72

training of word embeddings, which can leverage large amounts of unlabeled data to produce reliable word representations.

4.3 Impact of unsupervised pre-training of word embeddings

In Table 8 we assess the impact of unsupervised pre-training of word embeddings in CharWNN performance for both SPA CoNLL-2002 and HAREM I (selective). The results were computed using the CoNLL-2002 evaluation script. When unsupervised pre-training is not used, the word embeddings are initialized by randomly sampling each value from an uniform distribution: $\mathcal{U}(-r, r)$, where $r = \sqrt{\frac{6}{|V^{wrd}| + d^{wrd}}}$.

We can see in Table 8 that, for both corpora, CharWNN results are improved when using unsupervised pre-training. The impact of unsupervised pre-training is larger for the HAREM I corpus (13.2 points in the F1) than for the SPA CoNLL-2002 (4.3 points in the F1). We believe one of the main reasons of this difference in the impact is the training set size, which is much smaller in the HAREM I corpus.

5 Related Work

Some recent work on deep learning for named entity recognition include Chen et al. (2010), Collobert et al. (2011) and Passos et al. (2014).

Chen et al. (2010) employ deep belief networks (DBN) to perform named entity categorization. In their system, they assume that the boundaries of all the entity mentions were previously identified, which makes their task easier than the one we tackle in this paper. The input for their model is the character-level information of the entity to be classified. They apply their system for a Chinese corpus and achieve state-of-the-art results for the NE categorization task.

Collobert et al. (2011) propose a deep neural network which is equivalent to the WNN architecture described in Section 3.3. They achieve state-of-the-art results for English NER by adding a feature based on gazetteer information.

Passos et al. (2014) extend the Skip-Gram language model (Mikolov et al., 2013) to produce *phrase embeddings* that are more suitable to be used in a linear-chain CRF to perform NER. Their linear-chain CRF, which also uses additional handcrafted features such as gazetteer

Table 7: Results by entity type for the HAREM I corpus.

Entity	CharWNN			ETL_{CMT}		
	Prec.	**Rec.**	**F1**	**Prec.**	**Rec.**	**F1**
DATE	90.27	81.32	85.56	88.29	82.21	85.14
LOC	76.91	78.55	77.72	76.18	68.16	71.95
ORG	70.65	71.56	71.10	65.34	50.29	56.84
PER	81.35	77.07	79.15	81.49	61.14	69.87
VALUE	78.08	74.99	76.51	77.72	70.13	73.73
Overall	78.38	77.49	77.93	77.27	65.20	70.72

Table 8: Impact of unsup. pre-training of word emb. in CharWNN performance.

Corpus	Pre-trained word emb.	**Precision**	**Recall**	**F1**
SPA CoNLL-2002	Yes	**82.21**	**82.21**	**82.21**
	No	78.21	77.63	77.92
HAREM I	Yes	**73.98**	**68.68**	**71.23**
	No	65.21	52.27	58.03

based, achieves state-of-the-art results on two English corpora: CoNLL 2003 and Ontonotes NER.

The main difference between our approach and the ones proposed in previous work is the use of neural character embeddings. This type of embedding allows us to achieve state-of-the-art results for the full task of identifying and classifying named entities using only features automatically learned. Additionally, we perform experiments with two different languages, while previous work focused in one language.

6 Conclusions

In this work we approach language-independent NER using a DNN that employs word- and character-level embeddings to perform sequential classification. We demonstrate that the same DNN which was successfully applied for POS tagging can also achieve state-of-the-art results for NER, using the same hyperparameters, and without any handcrafted features. Moreover, we shed some light on the contribution of neural character embeddings for NER; and define new state-of-the-art results for two NER corpora in two different languages: Portuguese and Spanish.

Acknowledgments

Victor Guimarães' contributions were made during an internship at IBM Research.

References

James Bergstra, Olivier Breuleux, Frédéric Bastien, Pascal Lamblin, Razvan Pascanu, Guillaume Desjardins, Joseph Turian, David Warde-Farley, and Yoshua Bengio. 2010. Theano: a CPU and GPU math expression compiler. In *Proceedings of the Python for Scientific Computing Conference (SciPy)*.

Xavier Carreras, Lluís Màrques, and Lluís Padró. 2002. Named entity extraction using adaboost. In *Proceedings of CoNLL-2002*, pages 167–170. Taipei, Taiwan.

Yu Chen, You Ouyang, Wenjie Li, Dequan Zheng, and Tiejun Zhao. 2010. Using deep belief nets for chinese named entity categorization. In *Proceedings of the Named Entities Workshop*, pages 102–109.

R. Collobert, J. Weston, L. Bottou, M. Karlen, K. Kavukcuoglu, and P. Kuksa. 2011. Natural language processing (almost) from scratch. *Journal of Machine Learning Research*, 12:2493–2537.

R. Collobert. 2011. Deep learning for efficient discriminative parsing. In *Proceedings of the Fourteenth International Conference on Artificial Intelligence and Statistics (AISTATS)*, pages 224–232.

George Doddington, Alexis Mitchell, Mark Przybocki, Lance Ramshaw, Stephanie Strassel, and Ralph Weischedel. 2004. The automatic content extraction (ace) program tasks, data, and evaluation. In *Proceedings of the Fourth International Conference on Language Resources and Evaluation (LREC-2004)*, Lisbon, Portugal, May.

Cícero Nogueira dos Santos and Ruy Luiz Milidiú, 2012. *Entropy Guided Transformation Learning: Algorithms and Applications*, chapter Named entity recognition, pages 51–58. Springer Briefs in Computer Science. Springer.

Cícero Nogueira dos Santos and Bianca Zadrozny. 2014a. Learning character-level representations for part-of-speech tagging. In *Proceedings of the 31st International Conference on Machine Learning, JMLR: W&CP volume 32*, Beijing, China.

Cícero Nogueira dos Santos and Bianca Zadrozny. 2014b. Training state-of-the-art portuguese POS taggers without handcrafted features. In *Proceedings of the 11th International Conference Computational Processing of the Portuguese Language*, pages 82–93, São Carlos, Brazil.

Jenny Rose Finkel, Trond Grenager, and Christopher Manning. 2005. Incorporating non-local information into information extraction systems by gibbs sampling. In *Proceedings of the 43rd Annual Meeting on Association for Computational Linguistics*, pages 363–370.

Yann Lecun, Lon Bottou, Yoshua Bengio, and Patrick Haffner. 1998. Gradient-based learning applied to document recognition. In *Proceedings of the IEEE*, pages 2278–2324.

Tomas Mikolov, Kai Chen, Greg Corrado, and Jeffrey Dean. 2013. Efficient estimation of word representations in vector space. In *Proceedings of Workshop at International Conference on Learning Representations*.

Ruy Luiz Milidiú, Julio Cesar Duarte, and Roberto Cavalcante. 2007. Machine learning algorithms for portuguese named entity recognition. *Revista Iberoamericana de Inteligencia Artificial*, pages 67–75.

Alexandre Passos, Vineet Kumar, and Andrew McCallum. 2014. Lexicon infused phrase embeddings for named entity resolution. In *Proceedings of the Eighteenth Conference on Computational Natural Language Learning*, pages 78–86, Ann Arbor, Michigan.

Diana Santos and Nuno Cardoso. 2007. *Reconhecimento de entidades mencionadas em português*. Linguateca, Portugal.

Buzhou Tang, Hongxin Cao, Xiaolong Wang, Qingcai Chen, and Hua Xu. 2014. Evaluating word representation features in biomedical named entity recognition tasks. *BioMed Research International*, 2014.

Erik F. Tjong Kim Sang and Fien De Meulder. 2003. Introduction to the conll-2003 shared task: Language-independent named entity recognition. In Walter Daelemans and Miles Osborne, editors, *Proceedings of CoNLL-2003*, pages 142–147. Edmonton, Canada.

Erik F. Tjong Kim Sang. 2002. Introduction to the conll-2002 shared task: Language-independent named entity recognition. In *Proceedings of CoNLL-2002*, pages 155–158. Taipei, Taiwan.

A. J. Viterbi. 1967. Error bounds for convolutional codes and an asymptotically optimum decoding algorithm. *IEEE Transactions on Information Theory*, 13(2):260–269, April.

A. Waibel, T. Hanazawa, G. Hinton, K. Shikano, and K. J. Lang. 1989. Phoneme recognition using time-delay neural networks. *IEEE Transactions on Acoustics, Speech and Signal Processing*, 37(3):328–339.

Regularity and Flexibility in English-Chinese Name Transliteration

Oi Yee Kwong
Department of Translation
The Chinese University of Hong Kong
Shatin, N.T., Hong Kong
oykwong@arts.cuhk.edu.hk

Abstract

This paper reflects on the nature of English-Chinese personal name transliteration and the limitations of state-of-the-art language-independent automatic transliteration generation systems. English-Chinese name pairs from various sources were analysed and the complex interaction of factors in transliteration is discussed. Proposals are made for fuller error analysis in shared tasks and for expanding transliteration systems for computer-aided translation with an integrated model.

1 Introduction

Name transliteration is defined as the rendition of a name originating from a source language in a target language, such that its representation in the target language (i) is phonemically equivalent to the source name, (ii) conforms to the phonology of the target language, and (iii) matches the user intuition of the equivalent of the source language name in the target language, considering the culture and orthographic character usage in the target language. Such a definition has been adopted in the NEWS shared task on transliteration generation since 2009 (Li et al., 2009).

Automatic transliteration, or transliteration generation, has to do with the production of a transliterated name for a given source name by a trained system. Criteria (i) and (ii) above are relatively straightforward and are often the primary, if not only, concerns between most language pairs. For instance, the English name Clinton is rendered in Japanese by katakana as クリントン (ku-ri-n-to-n). The Japanese form is entirely based on phonemic resemblance as individual characters bear no particular meanings. For this reason, the correspondence is very likely to be unambiguous as long as the pronunciation is correctly figured out. Criterion (iii) above originally intends to ensure the usefulness of transliteration for downstream applications, in case the normal or expected form of the target name slightly violates the other two criteria. Nevertheless, this third criterion also applies quite specifically to target languages like Chinese. With its ideographic nature, each character does not only bear a phonetic but more importantly also a semantic component. This implies multiple possibilities for representing a particular phoneme, and consequently leads to the problem of character selection in transliteration. With the example of Clinton, the Chinese forms 克林頓 (Hanyu Pinyin: ke4-lin2-dun4) and 柯林頓 (ke1-lin2-dun4), bearing almost the same pronunciation in Mandarin Chinese, are thus both acceptable, while other homophonic forms like 刻林頓 (ke4-lin2-dun4) and 課林頓 (ke4-lin2-dun4) are not normally used.

Hence, for English-Chinese transliteration, there is obviously much greater flexibility which also encompasses a certain degree of regularity. The relatively free combination of characters in Chinese proper names is not a random phenomenon. In this paper, we show that beyond phonemic consideration, English-Chinese transliteration is actually governed by a complex but systematic interaction of various linguistic, social, cognitive, and cultural factors. Current evaluation metrics thus have limitations. With their underlying assumptions, they are good for evaluating the usefulness of transliteration systems for language processing applications, but they may not be adequate to accommodate the

Proceedings of the Fifth Named Entity Workshop, joint with 53rd ACL and the 7th IJCNLP, pages 34–42,
Beijing, China, July 26-31, 2015. ©2015 Association for Computational Linguistics

whole range of possibilities which may be more appreciated by actual translation tasks. We therefore propose deeper error analysis in transliteration evaluation, and an integrated model for transliteration.

Section 2 reviews related work. Section 3 describes the data sources for our analysis. Section 4 presents general observations for English-Chinese personal name transliteration, substantiated with quantitative comparisons in Section 5 with respect to various factors. In Section 6, deeper error analysis and an integrated model of name transliteration for computer-aided translation are proposed, followed by a conclusion with future work in Section 7.

2 Related Work

There are basically two categories of work on machine transliteration. On the one hand, various alignment models are used for acquiring transliteration lexicons from parallel corpora and other resources (e.g. Lee et al., 2006; Jin et al., 2008; Kuo and Li, 2008). On the other hand, statistical transliteration models are built for transliterating personal names and other proper names, and these models can be based on phonemes (e.g. Knight and Graehl, 1998; Virga and Khudanpur, 2003), graphemes (e.g. Li et al., 2004), or their combination (e.g. Oh and Choi, 2005). They may operate on characters (e.g. Shishtla et al., 2009), syllables (e.g. Wutiwiwatchai and Thangthai, 2010), as well as hybrid units (e.g. Oh and Choi, 2005). In addition to phonetic features, others like temporal, semantic, and tonal features have also been found useful in transliteration (e.g. Tao et al., 2006; Li et al., 2007; Yoon et al., 2007; Kwong, 2009).

The baseline in current English-Chinese transliteration generation research often refers to Li et al. (2004). They used a Joint Source-Channel Model under the direct orthographic mapping (DOM) framework, which skips the middle phonemic representation in conventional phoneme-based methods, and models the segmentation and alignment preferences by means of contextual n-grams of the transliteration units. Their method was shown to outperform phoneme-based methods and those based on the noisy channel model. In fact, transliteration of foreign names into Chinese is often based on the surface orthographic forms, as exemplified in the transliteration of Beckham, where the supposedly silent h in "ham" is taken as pronounced, resulting in 漢姆 (Hanyu Pinyin: han4-mu3) in Mandarin Chinese and 咸 (Jyutping: haam4) in Cantonese.

The reports of the shared task in NEWS 2009 (Li et al., 2009) and NEWS 2010 (Li et al., 2010) highlighted two particularly popular approaches for transliteration generation among the participating systems. One is phrase-based statistical machine transliteration (e.g. Song et al., 2010; Finch and Sumita, 2010) and the other is Conditional Random Fields which treats the task as one of sequence labelling (e.g. Shishtla et al., 2009). More recent shared tasks have shown a wider array of promising techniques (Zhang et al., 2011; Zhang et al., 2012), although the absolute results as measured by Word Accuracy in Top-1 (ACC), Fuzziness in Top-1 (Mean F-score), and Mean Reciprocal Rank (MRR) have not really demonstrated any remarkable boost.

3 Resources

English and Chinese personal names obtained from various resources were analysed to illustrate the properties of Chinese naming practice and English-Chinese name transliteration. The datasets used in this study are described below.

3.1 Monolingual Chinese Names (N1)

About 40,000 distinct names written in Chinese, including authentic Chinese names (e.g. 胡錦濤 Hu Jintao, 曾蔭權 Donald Tsang) and those transliterated from foreign origins (e.g. 克林頓 Bill Clinton, 奧尼爾 Shaquille O'Neal), were obtained from the Hong Kong, Beijing and Taipei sub-corpora of the LIVAC synchronous corpus [1] (Tsou and Lai, 2003). Names from Japanese and Korean (e.g. 酒井法子 Noriko Sakai, 金大中 Kim Dae-jung) and code-mixed names (e.g. C 朗拿度 Cristiano Ronaldo, A 卡達 Anthony Carter) were excluded. Since the names are personalities appearing on news media in the various places, there are overlaps but we assume that local names also occupy a substantial proportion in each place respectively.

3.2 English-Chinese Name Pairs (N2)

About 20,000 bilingual (English-Chinese) name pairs have been manually collected from various

[1] The corpus has been word segmented and annotated with part of speech (POS). The names were extracted with the relevant POS tag.

sources including the Internet, name dictionaries, and books on naming practice. These names cover commonly used given names, big names in history, and contemporary personalities in politics, sports, entertainment, and other fields. The data were pre-processed and categorised according to:

- Region of transliteration: Hong Kong, Mainland China, or Taiwan region
- Domain: politics, sports, entertainment, or others
- Gender (if known): male or female
- Name type (if known): last name or given name

This collection was organised into sub-datasets, two of which were used in the current study. Dataset N2a is a parallel collection containing transliterations from the three Chinese speech communities for a common set of English names, mostly for celebrities. Dataset N2b consists of the transliterations for a set of common English given names, for both male and female, used predominantly in Mainland China and Taiwan region respectively. The transliterated names were also automatically mapped to Hanyu Pinyin and Jyutping for their pronunciations in Mandarin and Cantonese respectively. The mappings were manually verified.

4 General Observations

Transliteration of foreign names can lead to different possibilities across various Chinese speech communities. Phonemic equivalence is often considered with Cantonese pronunciation in Hong Kong, and Mandarin pronunciation in Mainland China and Taiwan region. This difference in pronunciation has led to very observable differences in the choice of characters, not only between Cantonese and Mandarin speaking communities, but also even between Mandarin speaking communities as in Mainland China and Taiwan region. For example, the English segment "son" as in Richardson is often rendered as 臣 (Jyutping: san4; Hanyu Pinyin: chen2) in Hong Kong, but always as 森 (Hanyu Pinyin: sen1; Jyutping: sam1) in Mainland China and 遜 (Hanyu Pinyin: xun4; Jyutping: seon3) in Taiwan region[2]. The difference in phonological properties between Mandarin and Cantonese also leads to noticeable differences in syllabification. For example, extra syllables are often introduced for certain consonant segments in the middle of an English name, as in Hamilton, transliterated as 漢密爾頓 (Hanyu Pinyin: han4-mi4-er3-dun4) in Mainland China but 咸美頓 (Jyutping: haam4-mei5-deon6) in Hong Kong. The abundance of homophones and significance of tones in Chinese also introduces much more variability, thus Rivaldo could be acceptably transliterated as 里華度 (Jyutping: lei5-waa4-dou6) or 李華度 (Jyutping: lei5-waa4-dou6). Both forms have exactly the same pronunciation except that the first may more readily suggest that it is a foreign name while the second starts with a character which is also a common Chinese surname. The phonological context embedding a particular English segment also influences the pronunciation of the segment and thus the choice of Chinese characters. Such graphemic ambiguity is an important element in transliteration.

The domain in which a personality is active often plays a role in name transliteration. For instance, names of foreign stars in the showbiz are usually fully transliterated, with given names followed by last names, e.g. Julia Roberts is known as 茱莉亞蘿拔絲 (Jyutping: zyu1-lei6-aa3-lo4-bat6-si1) in Hong Kong. On the contrary, sports stars and people in politics are often only known by their transliterated last names, such as Wayne Rooney and Bill Clinton, which usually only appear as 朗尼 (Jyutping: long5-nei4) and 克林頓 (Jyutping: haak1-lam4-deon6) in Hong Kong. In addition, the gender of the person can somehow be reflected from the transliteration via character choice among homophones. In the case of Julia Roberts, the characters 茱, 莉, 蘿 and 絲 very strongly suggest the female gender, as the first three characters all relate to flowers and plants, and the fourth character relates to silk. This practice serves to meet the social and cultural preference

[2] Both Cantonese and Mandarin pronunciations, in Jyutping and Hanyu Pinyin respectively, are given for these examples so that the readers can have some idea of their difference. For the examples in the rest of this paper, only the relevant pronunciation will be shown, according to the region in which the transliterations are used.

and the cognitive expectation of the perceivers, and it seems to be more seriously observed in Hong Kong and Taiwan region. Transliterations in Mainland China often stick quite strictly to the pronunciation, and tend to be more gender-neutral especially when only last names are transliterated. For example, the Danish tennis player Caroline Wozniacki is known by most Hong Kong media as 禾絲妮雅琪 (Jyutping: wo4-si1-nei4-ngaa5-kei4) but as 沃伊尼亞茨基 (Hanyu Pinyin: wo4-yi1-ni2-ya4-ci2-ji1) by Mainland media. The former is apparently more feminine, as the characters 絲, 妮, 雅 and 琪 are predominantly used for female names.

These general observations thus suggest that in addition to phonemic resemblance, English-Chinese name transliteration is a result of the interaction among different factors which could be linguistic, social, cognitive, and cultural in nature. In the following we will look into these factors more thoroughly with our collected data.

The interplay of these factors means that English-Chinese transliteration enjoys much more flexibility, while this freedom is accompanied by a certain degree of regularity. It also points to the need for cautious interpretation of transliteration results measured by common evaluation metrics like ACC, Mean F-score and MRR. They are based on two assumptions. One is treating the transliteration task as a closed-set problem, and the other is pre-supposing a standard reference set of "correct" transliterations. These assumptions would be reasonable and realistic for language pairs where phonemic resemblance is the entire consideration. For English-Chinese name transliteration, however, these assumptions do not take into account the possibility and acceptability (and creativity) beyond those phonemically neutral and conventional transliterations. These limitations have to be fully realised so as to perceive the performance of individual systems in a fair way.

5 Beyond Phonemic Resemblance

English-Chinese transliteration is not different from transliteration between other language pairs as phonemic resemblance is still the foremost consideration, and in this regard objective system evaluation is feasible. However, the abundance of homophones makes the naming process so much more flexible that the space for "correct" transliteration is considerably, though not unlimitedly, expanded.

5.1 Character Choice and Culture

To start with, we look at the characters often used in personal names. With the Hong Kong data in Dataset N1, we took all three-character names with Chinese origin and all foreign transliterated names, and compared the most frequent characters used in them. For the Chinese names, we only considered the second and third characters, ignoring the last names for the current comparison. Table 1 shows the top 30 characters used in the two kinds of names. It is very obvious that Chinese names and transliterated names appearing in Hong Kong media are composed of very different characters. This is possibly a result of the different phonology between English and Chinese, and thus very different pronunciations or sounds are found, leading to the use of characters in transliterated names which are not commonly found in traditional Chinese names. Among the top 100 characters in both kinds of names, only 10 characters were found in common: 德 (dak1), 亞 (aa3), 維 (wai4), 基 (gei1), 世 (sai3), 林 (lam4), 安 (ngon1), 金 (gam1), 文 (man4), and 海 (hoi2).

A similar comparison was done on the Mainland China and Taiwan region data in Dataset N1, and a similar difference between the characters used for Chinese names and transliterated names is observed. For instance, within the top 100 characters, 12% and 11% overlap were observed for Mainland China data and Taiwan region data respectively. The common characters between the two types of names in Mainland China are 德 (de2), 克 (ke4), 維 (wei2), 亞 (ya4), 基 (ji1), 林 (lin2), 安 (an1), 梅 (mei2), 金 (jin1), 文 (wen2), 小 (xiao3), and 海 (hai3); while those for the Taiwan region are 德 (de2), 瑞 (rui4), 維 (wei2), 達 (da2), 安 (an1), 吉 (ji2), 傑 (jie2), 林 (lin2), 雅 (ya3), 金 (jin1), and 華 (hua2).

Comparing the characters used for transliterated names among the three regions, it is apparent that Hong Kong and Mainland China tend to use more similar characters (although the precise syllabification and correspondence between English and Chinese segments might be different, as discussed in Section 5.2 below), while Taiwan region has a somewhat different character choice. Table 2 shows the commonality and difference among the three communities with respect to the top 100 characters in individual regions.

No.	HK Chinese	HK Foreign	No.	HK Chinese	HK Foreign
1	國	斯	16	英	布
2	文	爾	17	東	阿
3	華	德	18	雄	納
4	明	拉	19	生	巴
5	志	克	20	清	科
6	建	特	21	家	迪
7	德	夫	22	仁	亞
8	永	里	23	小	森
9	偉	羅	24	輝	伊
10	光	卡	25	中	維
11	平	利	26	林	姆
12	榮	馬	27	麗	雷
13	強	尼	28	金	普
14	玉	哈	29	慶	米
15	成	格	30	昌	基

Table 1: Top 30 characters used in Chinese and transliterated names from Dataset N1 (HK)

Comparison \ Region	Hong Kong	Mainland China	Taiwan region
Common	斯 克 爾 拉 特 德 尼 卡 羅 夫 里 布 艾 諾 利 馬 巴 格 維 洛 亞 阿 納 茲 哈 西 迪 麥 森 曼 達 普 塔 安 雷 魯 瓦 貝 伊 吉 恩 米 希 蘭 波 姆 威 奇 莫 萊 伯 勒 沙 薩 凱 基 比 托 倫 索 多 蒂 塞 林 法 奧 蘇 梅 杜 頓 科 金 帕 菲 赫 耶 費 加 穆		
Unique	世 高 二 盧	什 蒙 小 朗 茨	瑞 絲 莉 歐 柯 佛 瑪 葛 提 娜 柏 傑 妮 可 雅 莎 華 賈 丹 娃

Table 2: Comparison of character choice in individual communities from Dataset N1

5.2 Linguistic Factors

According to Dobrovolsky and Katamba (1996), native speakers of any language intuitively know that certain words that come from other languages sound unusual and they often adjust the segment sequences of these words to conform to the pronunciation requirements of their own language. These intuitions are based on a tacit knowledge of the permissible syllable structures of the speaker's own language. The difference between transliterations based on Mandarin and Cantonese is particularly obvious between Mainland China and Hong Kong, where the resulting number of syllables in the transliterated names is on average higher for the former. With Dataset N2a, we can compare the regional differences with respect to a more or less common set of transliterated names.

Among the common set of names, it was found that the average number of syllables (which correspond to the Chinese characters) is 2.60, 2.88, and 2.74 for Hong Kong, Mainland China, and Taiwan region respectively. This is mostly due to phonological differences. English and Chinese have very different phonological properties. A well cited example is a syllable initial /d/ may surface as in Baghdad 巴格達 (Hanyu Pinyin: ba1-ge2-da2), but the syllable final /d/ is not represented. This is true for Mandarin Chinese, but since ending stops like -p, -t, and -k are allowed in Cantonese syllables, the syllable final /d/ in Baghdad is already captured in the last syllable of 巴格達 (Jyutping: baa1-gaak3-daat6) in Cantonese. This difference in allowable codas sometimes surfaces in the form of an additional syllable in transliterations based on Mandarin. For example, Dickson is transliterated as 迪克遜 (Hanyu Pinyin: di2-ke4-xun4) in Mandarin Chinese and 迪臣 (Jyutping: dik6-san4) in Cantonese, where no extra syllable is introduced in the latter. This possibly accounts for the greater number of syllables for transliterations found in Mainland China and Taiwan region, as both these communities transliterate by Mandarin pronunciations. This is also reflected in the top English-Chinese segment pairs found from the three places, as shown in Table 3. From the table, we can see that English segments like "D", "T", "C", and "K" occupy the top positions for Mainland China and Taiwan region, where they consistently demand an additional syllable in the transliteration based on Mandarin. Although the corresponding segments are sometimes found in Hong Kong transliterations, they are nevertheless not as apparent and frequent.

As far as intra-regional variability is concerned, it is interesting to note that there are 1,974 distinct English-Chinese segment pairs in the Hong Kong data, but only 1,411 and 1,734 distinct pairs in the Mainland China and Taiwan region data respectively. This suggests that transliterations in Mainland China are most consistent, if not perfectly standardised. For instance, in the *Chinese Transliteration of Foreign Personal Names* published by the Xinhua News Agency (1992), a table showing the prescriptive Chinese rendition of individual English syllables is included. Transliterations in Hong Kong, however, are much more variable, and there are many ways to render a particular syllable.

No.	Hong Kong		Mainland China		Taiwan Region	
1	S	斯	S	斯	S	斯
2	SON	遜	L	爾	D	德
3	S	史	D	德	T	特
4	L	爾	T	特	K	克
5	TON	頓	C	克	B	布
6	G	格	SON	森	SON	森
7	O	奧	RI	里	C	克
8	A	亞	B	布	S	史
9	A	艾	G	格	RO	羅
10	BA	巴	K	克	TON	頓

Table 3: Top 10 English-Chinese segment pairs from Dataset N2a

5.3 Cognitive Factors

There are only a few hundred Chinese characters commonly used in transliterated names. Although their choice and combination are relatively free, the flexibility is not entirely ungoverned. For instance, the former Brazilian striker Ronaldo is typically rendered as 朗拿度 (Jyutping: long5-naa4-dou6) in Cantonese, but never as phonetically equivalent candidates like 朗娜度 (Jyutping: long5-naa4-dou6) or 郎拿刀 (Jyutping: long4-naa4-dou1). In this example, the second candidate is not preferred, as 娜 is conventionally restricted to female names (further discussed in Section 5.4 below). The third candidate is also not suitable. Even though 郎 is masculine, 刀 is probably not a character with enough positive meanings and is only occasionally found in Chinese names. This consideration in character choice is apparently cognitively based, with regard to the positive and negative connotations of individual characters, and thus their suitability for names. Apart from that, cognitive factors may involve the intonation of a name, which may also make a difference in the preference of a name. In particular, Chinese is a typical tonal language. Cantonese, in particular, has more tones than Mandarin, and the sound-tone combination is more important in names pronounced in Cantonese. Names which sound "nice" (or more "musical") are often preferred to those which sound "monotonous". It is thus important to consider the tone combination in transliteration. To this end, Kwong (2009) has shown that the improvement from including tones in a Joint Source-Channel model for automatic transliteration was more apparent for Cantonese data.

5.4 Social Factors

Gender difference is often reflected in the character choice for the transliterated names. Table 4 shows the most frequent characters for transliterating male and female given names in Mainland China and Taiwan region as analysed from Dataset N2b.

No.	Mainland China		Taiwan Region	
	Male	Female	Male	Female
1	斯	娜	斯	莉
2	爾	麗	爾	娜
3	里	莉	克	拉
4	特	拉	瑞	絲
5	德	爾	德	妮
6	克	特	特	瑪
7	利	絲	艾	西
8	尼	妮	尼	琳
9	羅	德	羅	安
10	雷	婭	利	凱

Table 4: Top 10 characters for male and female names in Dataset N2b

In terms of gender difference, the character sets are quite different for male and female names, in both regions alike. For instance, 219 and 256 distinct Chinese characters were found for female names and male names respectively from the Mainland China data, with 174 characters in common. For Taiwan region data, 230 and 275 distinct Chinese characters were found for female names and male names respectively, with only 136 characters in common. In other words, it suggests that the gender difference is much more apparent and significant for transliterations in Taiwan region, whereas transliterations in Mainland China tend to use more gender-neutral characters (as already shown in the example of Wozniacki earlier).

The actual characters used in transliteration in both regions are also considerably different. For instance, among the 219 and 230 characters for female names in Mainland China and Taiwan region respectively, 139 are in common (that is, around 60%); whereas among the 256 and 275 characters for males names in the two places respectively, 199 characters are in common (that is, over 70%). Hence the difference between the two regions is greater in the transliteration of female names than that of male names.

Table 5 shows an example for the English segment "LI". It is obvious that the general graphemic and homophone ambiguity can somehow be reduced when gender is taken into account. For instance, 莉 (li4) and 麗 (li4) are mostly restricted to female names, whereas 力 (li4) and 立 (li4) are predominantly used for male names. Others like 利 (li4) and 里 (li3) are more or less gender-neutral.

The ability to distinguish the gender from the transliterated name is particularly useful as it could help resolve ambiguity in translation especially when there are more than one possible candidate bearing the same last name, such as John Williams the musician and Venus Williams the woman tennis player. The gender factor in transliteration thus bears important implications not only in (back) transliteration but also in translation in general.

	Male	**Female**
Mainland China	利 (Cliff 克利夫) 里 (Ali 阿里) 萊 (Clive 克萊夫)	利 (Melissa 梅利莎) 里 (Ali 阿里) 莉 (Alisha 阿莉莎) 萊 (Carolina 卡羅萊娜) 麗 (Alice 艾麗斯)
Taiwan Region	力 (Philip 菲力普) 立 (Oliver 奧立佛) 利 (Julian 朱利安) 里 (Cliff 克里夫) 萊 (Linus 萊納斯) 賴 (Elijah 伊賴嘉)	里 (Celia 賽里雅) 莉 (Alisha 艾莉夏) 琳 (Carolina 卡蘿琳娜) 麗 (Lisa 麗莎)

Table 5: Examples of gender-specific rendition of the English segment "LI" from Dataset N2b

Thus in this section, we have discussed the impact of various factors on English-Chinese personal name transliteration with empirical evidence. In particular, we have investigated the complex interaction among syllabification, phonological difference, homophones, tones, gender, and domain, in transliteration across three Chinese speech communities, namely Hong Kong, Mainland China, and Taiwan region.

6 Proposals

6.1 Deeper Error Analysis

With the current paradigm adopted in the shared task on transliteration generation, systems are evaluated by how often the first-ranked transliteration generated by a system matches the "answer" given in the evaluation data, and on average when will the "answer" appear in the top 10 transliterations given by the system. In terms of providing a common platform for evaluation, this is a natural and reasonable approach. However, it should not be disregarded that even if the system-generated result is not exactly the same as that in the evaluation data, it does not necessarily mean it is "wrong" or useless. As discussed above, English-Chinese name transliteration involves the interaction of linguistic, cognitive, social and cultural factors, and multiple renditions could be considered acceptable. Thus, usually there is no right or wrong, but better or worse, for the system-generated transliteration candidates.

In fact, when we look at the evaluation results over the last few shared tasks, there is no remarkable breakthrough observed. Literally the figures seem to be deteriorating. Considering the system with top performance in the English-Chinese transliteration task (standard run), the ACC, F-score and MRR were 0.731, 0.895 and 0.812 respectively in 2009. In 2010, they are 0.477, 0.740 and 0.506 respectively. In 2011, they are 0.349, 0.700 and 0.462 respectively. In 2012, they are 0.330, 0.669 and 0.413 respectively.

It will certainly be unfair to compare the above figures directly since different datasets were used, but the situation also raises the issue of robustness. The shared task for this year is re-using the test data from one of the previous years in order to track system improvement. [3] In addition to this, we suggest that deeper error analysis would be useful to obtain a better idea of the limitation of state-of-the-art system performance. It would be important to find out whether the bottleneck is possibly caused by the difference in training data, and whether the "unmatched" transliteration candidates could

[3] According to the shared task results provided by one of the anonymous reviewers, results for standard runs in the EnCh task do not seem to demonstrate any remarkable improvement. Further information and discussion are expected with the release of the official analysis and comparison.

also be considered acceptable; or otherwise what might have led to their unacceptability. For instance, the inexact matches generated by systems could be further analysed and classified according to the nature of the "errors", such as phonemic non-equivalence, character mismatch, character misuse, unseen characters, tone problem or perceptual idiosyncrasy, and region compatibility, just to name a few possibilities. It will be worthwhile to pursue such a direction in future evaluation of machine transliteration, while a similar need to augment automatic metric with linguistic and perceptual considerations for machine translation evaluation has been realised and proposed by Farrús et al. (2012). One of the primary concerns would naturally be the balance between automatic and manual work to be involved in the whole evaluation process.

6.2 An Integrated Model

The ability for systems to produce linguistically and cognitively acceptable transliterations is particularly important. New names or unseen names appear every day in the media, and accurate and reasonable renditions of foreign names into Chinese will be very useful, not only for downstream language processing applications, but also as a significant component for computer-aided translation in practice. Transliteration is to render a source name in a phonemically similar way in a target language. The linguistic factors, considering the phonological properties of the two languages and thus the syllabification, should bear primary importance. Other interacting factors, including the intonation, gender difference, and domain, may be considered peripheral, but considering them would certainly help produce better perceived candidates. For the case of English-Chinese transliteration, the cultural differences must not be ignored. They must be taken into account to ensure that the resulting transliterations are intelligible and appropriate to the Chinese speakers in individual regions.

An integrated model for transliteration is therefore necessary, although this might be at the expense of a completely language-independent design. We propose that a transliteration system should contain three major components, for segmentation, candidate generation, and candidate ranking respectively. The segmentation module should consist of a linguistic model, to break up a source name into pronunciation segments. The linguistic model incorporates language-specific phonological properties (for both the source language and target language), for initial syllabification of the source name and reconstructing the segmentation structure into one which is compatible with the requirements of the target language. The candidate generation module should consist of a cultural model, which provides information on the naming practice adopted in various cultures and the range of orthographic renditions usually allowed for personal names. The candidate ranking module should consist of a social module to compare the candidate transliterations for their desirability according to social factors like gender difference and domain preference, as well as a cognitive module to consider factors like pleasantness of sound and intonation, and avoidance of unfavourable homophone strings.

7 Conclusion and Future Work

In this paper, we have reflected on the nature of English-Chinese name transliteration, which is distinct from transliteration between other language pairs in its much greater flexibility beyond pure phonemic equivalence. A complex yet systematic interplay of cultural, linguistic, cognitive and social factors was shown from empirical data. On the one hand, we suggest that deeper error analysis of transliteration systems be performed to realise the limitations of common evaluation metrics. On the other hand, we propose an integrated model for a robust English-Chinese transliteration system. Practical systems, especially those for computer-aided translation, should consider the art and science of the transliteration task. In order to consider a realistically wider range of transliteration candidates, a system should take into account various interacting factors while capitalising on statistical patterns. The implementation of such a system will constitute an important part of our future work.

References

Dobrovolsky, M. and F. Katamba. 1996. Phonology: the function and patterning of sounds. In W. O'Grady, M. Dobrovolsky and F. Katamba (Eds.), *Contemporary Linguistics: An Introduction*. Essex: Addison Wesley Longman Limited.

Farrús, M., M.R. Costa-jussà and M. Popović. 2012. Study and Correlation Analysis of Linguistic, Perceptual, and Automatic Machine Translation Evaluations. *Journal of the American Society for Information Science and Technology, 63(1)*:174-184.

Finch, A. and E. Sumita. 2010. Transliteration using a phrase-based statistical machine translation system to re-score the output of a joint multigram model. In *Proceedings of NEWS 2010*, Uppsala, Sweden.

Jin, C., S-H. Na, D-I. Kim and J-H. Lee. 2008. Automatic Extraction of English-Chinese Transliteration Pairs using Dynamic Window and Tokenizer. In *Proceedings of the Sixth SIGHAN Workshop on Chinese Language Processing (SIGHAN-6)*, Hyderabad, India, pp.9-15.Katamba, F. 1989. *An Introduction to Phonology*. Essex: Longman Group UK Limited.

Knight, K. and J. Graehl. 1998. Machine Transliteration. *Computational Linguistics, 24(4)*:599-612.

Kuo, J-S. and H. Li. 2008. Mining Transliterations from Web Query Results: An Incremental Approach. In *Proceedings of the Sixth SIGHAN Workshop on Chinese Language Processing (SIGHAN-6)*, Hyderabad, India, pp.16-23.

Kwong, O.Y. 2009. Homophones and Tonal Patterns in English-Chinese Transliteration. In *Proceedings of the ACL-IJCNLP 2009 Conference Short Papers*, Singapore, pp.21-24.

Lee, C-J., J.S. Chang and J-S.R. Jang. 2006. Extraction of transliteration pairs from parallel corpora using a statistical transliteration model. *Information Sciences, 176*:67-90.

Li, H., A. Kumaran, V. Pervouchine and M. Zhang. 2009. Report of NEWS 2009 Machine Transliteration Shared task. In *Proceedings of NEWS 2009*, Singapore.

Li, H., A. Kumaran, M. Zhang and V. Pervouchine. 2010. Report of NEWS 2010 Transliteration Generation Shared Task. In *Proceedings of NEWS 2010*, Uppsala, Sweden.

Li, H., K.C. Sim, J-S. Kuo and M. Dong. 2007. Semantic Transliteration of Personal Names. In *Proceedings of ACL 2007*, Prague, Czech Republic, pp.120-127.

Li, H., M. Zhang and J. Su. 2004. A Joint Source-Channel Model for Machine Transliteration. In *Proceedings of ACL 2004*, Barcelona, Spain, pp.159-166.

Oh, J-H. and K-S. Choi. 2005. An Ensemble of Grapheme and Phoneme for Machine Transliteration. In R. Dale *et al.* (Eds.), *Natural Language Processing – IJCNLP 2005*. Springer, LNAI Vol. 3651, pp.451-461.

Shishtla, P., V.S. Ganesh, S. Sethuramalingam and V. Varma. 2009. A language-independent transliteration schema using character aligned models. In *Proceedings of NEWS 2009*, Singapore.

Song, Y., C. Kit and H. Zhao. 2010. Reranking with multiple features for better transliteration. In *Proceedings of NEWS 2010*, Uppsala, Sweden.

Tao, T., S-Y. Yoon, A. Fister, R. Sproat and C. Zhai. 2006. Unsupervised Named Entity Transliteration Using Temporal and Phonetic Correlation. In *Proceedings of EMNLP 2006*, Sydney, Australia, pp.250-257.

Tsou, B.K. 鄒嘉彥 and T.B.Y. Lai 黎邦洋. 2003. 漢語共時語料庫與資訊開發，《中文資訊處理若干重要問題》, pp.147-165. 北京:科學出版社.

Virga, P. and S. Khudanpur. 2003. Transliteration of Proper Names in Cross-lingual Information Retrieval. In *Proceedings of the ACL2003 Workshop on Multilingual and Mixed-language Named Entity Recognition*.

Wutiwiwatchai, C. and A. Thangthai. 2010. Syllable-based Thai-English Machine Transliteration. In *Proceedings of NEWS 2010*, Uppsala, Sweden, pp.66-70.

Xinhua News Agency. 1992. *Chinese Transliteration of Foreign Personal Names*. The Commercial Press.

Yoon, S-Y., K-Y. Kim and R. Sproat. 2007. Multilingual Transliteration Using Feature based Phonetic Method. In *Proceedings of the 45th Annual Meeting of the Association for Computational Linguistics (ACL 2007)*, Prague, Czech Republic, pp.112-119.

Zhang, M., H. Li, A. Kumaran and M. Liu. 2011. Report of NEWS 2011 Transliteration Generation Shared Task. In *Proceedings of NEWS 2011*, Chiang Mai, Thailand, pp.1-13.

Zhang, M., H. Li, A. Kumaran and M. Liu. 2012. Report of NEWS 2012 Machine Transliteration Shared task. In *Proceedings of NEWS 2012*, Jeju, Korea, pp.10-20.

HAREM and Klue: how to compare two tagsets for named entities annotation

Livy Real
IBM Research
livyreal@gmail.com

Alexandre Rademaker
IBM Research and FGV/EMAp
alexrad@br.ibm.com

Abstract

This paper describes an undergoing experiment to compare two tagsets for Named Entities (NE) annotation. We compared Klue 2 tagset, developed by IBM Research, with HAREM tagset, developed for tagging the Portuguese corpora used in Second HAREM competition. From this report, we expected to evaluate our methodology for comparison and to survey the problems that arise from it.

1 Introduction

Named-entity recognition (NER) is a subtask of many information extraction procedures. Its aims is to track and categorize pieces of texts (words, multiwords expressions, etc) into predefined classes such as the names of persons, organizations, etc. The state-of-the-art systems for English are able to produce near-human performance. In MUC-7 (Message Understanding Conference, 1998), the best system entering the joint evaluation scored 93.39% of F-measure while human annotators scored 97.6% and 96.95% (Perzanowski, 1998).

The good results achieved by some systems in MUC-7 don't mean that NER is entirely understood, mainly if we consider languages different from English. Moreover, to compare NER systems is a hard goal since the definition of what is a named entity itself is getting fuzzier and have passed to included not only proper nouns (Robinson, 1997). The decision to add dates, quantities or events to NE label, for example, makes necessary the retrieve of more information and is harder to keep the same score of recall and precision.

In most cases, NER is done through statistical or machine learning procedures. The IBM Statistical Information and Relation Extraction (SIRE) is one of such systems. It can be use to build trainable extractors for different domains. SIRE provides components for mention detection using Maximum Entropy models (Ratnaparkhi, 1998) that can be trained from annotated data created by using a highly optimized web-browser annotation tool, called HAT, a trainable co-reference component for grouping detected mentions in a document that correspond to the same entity, and a trainable relation extraction system.

The HAT annotation tool can be configure to use different tagset, which is also called type system, depending on the project. For news domain, a tagset named Klue was created. The Klue tagset was developed among several projects at IBM Research, mainly focused on annotate English articles with the goal extracted entities and relations between them. Therefore, Klue is a product of successive refinements, now in its third version.

After the introduction of Watson technology in the market, IBM is moving forward to make the systems adapted to work with other languages, not only English. The SIRE toolkit is part of the Watson ecosystem. Our project is to help on the improvement of SIRE models for Portuguese. Since annotated corpora were necessary to this task, we have developed an initial experiment to use an already available annotated Portuguese corpora to train a extractor model using SIRE. For this, we decide to use HAREM [1] gold collection, mapping the annotation from HAREM into Klue. Since SIRE achieves high F1 measures in many languages, this make us to believe that if we use a good annotated corpus in Portuguese, we could also obtain a good extractor using SIRE training module.

HAREM was a joint evaluation of NER system for Portuguese promoted by Linguateca, that had two editions so far. The tagset used in the gold collection of HAREM was created especially for the Second HAREM competition and it was the

[1] http://www.linguateca.pt/harem/

Proceedings of the Fifth Named Entity Workshop, joint with 53rd ACL and the 7th IJCNLP, pages 43–49,
Beijing, China, July 26-31, 2015. ©2015 Association for Computational Linguistics

result of an agreement between the competitors that shared the combination of the types that their systems were able to recognize. In other words, the HAREM tagset was not planned as a tagset with the goal of supporting information extraction in any particular project, instead it was built from the combination of the types that several systems could annotate.

This works aims to describe our attempt to evaluate how adequate a tagset created for annotate named entities occurrences in English texts is to annotate Portuguese texts. Although Klue tagset is supposed to be a language-independent tagset, the differences we found between Klue and HAREM type systems grew some important questions: (i) Can tagsets really be language-independent? (ii) Can we believe in a true universal tagset which capture NE from any language? (iii) Does it make sense to expect that they will be completely interchangeable?

For now, we are still working on these answers and analysing both Klue and HAREM tagsets under these thoughts. For sure, tagsets are more useful if they are created to a specific domain and project, in a specific language, to a specific textual genre, but the general attempt to reach an universal tagset is an imposed challenge, since most of the tools for Natural Language Processing (NLP) aim to be universal, i.e., they aim to work with many languages and to be interoperable.

We expect to achieve a straightforward methodology to compare and adapt two different tagsets for NER. Also, we expected that there problems when using Klue tagset into Portuguese data will arise. We'll attempt to produce an empirical overview of this kind of adaptation, that is common in NLP studies, but it is not so frequently considered.

This short paper is being written while the experiment is still undergoing, but we intend to report our experience so far and share ideas with the NER researchers community.

The work is presented as following: first we'll introduce Klue and HAREM. In Section 3.1 we'll describe our proposal for the comparison between them and present the issues we found, focusing on linguistic problems from multilingual perspective, and what we could learn until now from this experiment. Finally we'll discuss some possible conclusions from it and what we leave as future work.

2 SIRE and Klue

Klue stands for Knowledge from Language Understanding and Extraction and it is one type system created to be used with SIRE toolkit. SIRE implements the Maximum Entropy Modeling for Named Entities recognition (Ratnaparkhi, 1998).

The framework that uses Klue is described in (Florian et al., 2004) and, in the last two Automatic Content Extraction (ACE) evaluations, [2] achieved top-tier results in all three evaluation languages that is participated (English, Arabic and Chinese). In ACE'02, the IBM system achieved the best values for NE detection. It achieved a F-measure of 0.685 for Arabic, 0.686 for Chinese and 0.734 for English, which is very close to human performance on this task.

Klue is used to entities tag, but also to tag relations and co-reference between them, what gives to Klue a particular feature: named entities, or *mentions*, are understood as a more open concept which includes not only proper nouns, but also pronouns, values and verbs, as it is defined "actual words referring to a certain thing or interest". This feature makes of Klue a very expressive tagset when we compare with others type systems, because it is prepared to capture much more elements than what we usually call named entity. In the research, we used the version 2 of Klue tagset, called Klue 2.

Using KLUE, *Mentions*, after a POS tagger first trial, can be categorized into *entity types*, *roles* and *sub-types*. In that sense, *entity type* indicates what type of an entity a said mention refers to, without considering context. *Entity types* have context-free nature and every *mention* with the same spelling belongs to the same *entity type*. The contextual meanings of said mention is given trough *roles*: the context sensitive meaning of a *mention*. A*subtype* is a finer-grained typological information to *entities types* which can produces *subtypes*, following the architecture TYPE.SUBTYPE, which seems to be freely inspired by Generative Lexicon strategy (Pustejovsky, 1995). Table 1 list the Klue 2 entity types and sub-types.

3 HAREM

HAREM (Cardoso, 2008a) is a joint evaluation of entities mentioned recognition systems for Por-

[2] For a description of the ACE evaluation, see `http://www.nist.gov/speech/tests/ace/`.

age	animal	award
cardinal	date	degree
disease	duration	email
event	facility	food
geologicalobj	gpe	law
location	measure	money
ordinal	organ	organization
people	person	percent
personpeople	phone	plant
product	substance	ticker
time	titlework	vehicle
weapon	weather	web

Table 1: Klue 2 Types and Subtypes

tuguese organized by Linguateca team. [3] In short, it is an initiative that aims to evaluate the success in identifying and classifying proper names in Portuguese. The set of HAREM evaluations was made between 2004 and 2007.

These evaluations came from three instances of HAREM editions: First HAREM (2004-2006), Mini HAREM (2006) and Second HAREM (2006-2008). The differences between these three evaluations are deeply explained in (Cardoso, 2008a, p.1-7). Here we use the tagset and golden collection [4] from Second HAREM, an edition made only by lusophone scholars and whose labels regarding time are more consistent than in the previous evaluations.

The Second HAREM collection includes 1,040 documents covering Brazilian and European Portuguese. Its Golden Collection is a subset of it consisting in 129 documents (2,274 paragraphs; 147,991 words) which represents 12% of the general collection. It was manually annotated and deeply discussed and revised by the HAREM team.

An important feature of HAREM, when it is compared to Klue, is the assumption that the meaning of a NE is defined only in context and can not be lexically defined. This consequently results in the fact that a NE may be marked as belonging to more than one category, especially when the context is not enough to define its meaning.

Since HAREM defines named entities as proper nouns, a very vague definition, some criteria were used for identify NE. The criteria for tagging a named entity used by HAREM includes: capitalized words (as *Obama, Lula*), expressions of time (month, dates), address, treatment pronouns (such as *Lord, Mr.*) and what they call "abstraction" (such as *illness, state, syndrome*).

HAREM categorizes named entities into *Categoria* ('category'), *Tipo* ('type'), *Subtipo* ('subtype') and also offers to annotators other possible tags, not very used on the final evaluation, as *COREL* ('co-relation') and *TIPOREL* ('type relation').

Tagging in HAREM consists in assigning at least a *category* to a named entity. After it, *types* which belong to the assigned *category* can also be assigned on the named entity, as well as *subtypes* that belongs to the same tagged *type*. We can see the HAREM annotation on the example below: [5]

```
<p>Com a influencia do <ALT>
<EM ID="hub-83689-179"
    CATEG="PESSOA" TIPO="CARGO">
bispo de Burgos</EM>
|
bispo de
<EM ID="hub-83689-180" CATEG="LOCAL"
    TIPO="HUMANO" SUBTIPO="DIVISAO">
Burgos</EM>
</ALT>
conseguiram a aprovacao do projecto
por parte de
<EM ID="hub-83689-144" CATEG="PESSOA"
    TIPO="INDIVIDUAL">Carlos V</EM>.</p>
```

where we can see entities marked with `EM`, the tag `ALT` do signal alternative annotations. In each `EM` tag we have the attributes for `CAT`, `ID` and `TIPO`. The tag `p` is the HTML tag for paragraphs.

In Table 2, we present all HAREM *categories* and *types*, we did not include the *subtypes* in this table because they are too many and not so relevant to the present work.

The systems that participated on Second HAREM are CaGE2, DobrEM, PorTexTO, Priberam, R3M, REMBRANDT, REMMA 3, SEI-Geo, SeRELeP and XIP-L2F/XEROX. Second HAREM evaluation allowed each system to choose a different task (for example, one could choose which categories to tag), what, following the authors, makes it's evaluation a bit superficial. Nevertheless the main task (to recognize a named entity and correctly classify them) is the same for all participant systems. The system with the best F measure (0.5711) was Priberam system (Amaral, 2008), followed by REMBRANDT System (Cardoso, 2008b) with its better run achieving 0.5674 F measure. All the other systems did not get a F

[3] `http://www.linguateca.pt/`

[4] The set of documents used for training the models.

[5] 'The treaty of Tordesillas divided the world.'

Category	Type
abstraction	discipline
	state
	idea
	name
	other
happening	ephemeris
	event
	organized
	other
person	position
	positiongroup
	indgroup
	membergroup
	individual
	member
	people
	other
thing	class
	class member
	object
	substance
	other
location	physical
	human
	virtual
	other
work	art
	plan
	reproduced
	other
time	duration
	frequency
	generic
	calendar
	other
value	classification
	currency
	quantity
	other
other	

Table 2: HAREM - Categories and Types

measure value higher than 0.5.

3.1 Comparison

To produce a comparison between Klue and HAREM tagsets, we have started from HAREM, as the annotated corpus that we want to adapt already use HAREM golden collection. Since the tagsets use different architectures, we produced a mapping table focusing in the tagset used by HAREM.

In the mapping, if a *category.entitytype* from HAREM has a straightforward relation to an *entitytype* from Klue — as the case of VALUE.QUANTITY which tags the same set of NE than the Klue *entity type* MEASURE — it is tracked. If a *category.entitytype* from HAREM has a straightforward relation to an *entitytype.role* from Klue — as the case ORGANIZATION.COMPANY and ORGANIZATION.COMMERCIAL — it is also tracked.

The complete mapping in showed in the Table 3 in the end of this report. We use **various** whenever any of the following types can be used: ANIMAL, PRODUCT, LAW, ORGANIZATION, VEHICLE, WEAPON, OTHER.

Once the mapping from Table 3 is defined, the most difficult remain task to make the translation is to collect the annotations made in-line in the HAREM documents to construct the SIRE documents format. Although both formats adopt a XML-like style, Klue docx format does not mark annotations in-line with the text, the docx document format has a special section for mentions with references to the offsets (begin and end) in the text of each mention. [6]

4 Issues

The main problem we have to deal with is how these two tagsets treats named entities. HAREM uses the more basic definition, in other words, it focus on proper names. Klue is more interested in co-reference and relations, then it is a typology that also includes common nouns, pronouns and verbs. Many pairs *category.entity* from HAREM has a straightforward *entity type* in Klue (as the relation PERSON.INDIVIDUAL into PERSON), but many other have not. ABSTRACTION.IDEA, for example, does not have a correspondent in Klue. It happens the same to the OTHER.OTHER category in HAREM, as Klue does not have so open types, there is not relation to be tracked. Whenever there is not possible relation between something tagged by HAREM into Klue, we leave the correspondence blank and the named entities marked by HAREM as belongs to these categories are not considered by our work. The elements that are not under our comparison represents 6% of the entire HAREM corpus.

In another hand, the HAREM pair *THING.OBJECT* has many possible correspondent tags in Klue (as ANIMAL, PRODUCT, LAW, ORGANIZATION, VEHICLE, WEAPON or OTHER), since the criteria used by the two tagsets are different. HAREM categorizes as THING every object or animal which is not a person and by OBJECT things with names. Klue

[6] The code that we used to translate the HAREM documents to Klue documents is available at `https://github.com/arademaker/harem`.

does not have a 'thing' category and tag directly the mention as the function of it in the real world. How to solve it is maybe the main issue that arose for our automatic methodology, as the system can not automatically choose between all these possibilities which is the correct one and we tried to avoid manual annotation in this case.

The cited issues come from the different criteria adopted by the tagsets, but also some language specific issues arose. For example, the HAREM *category* PERSON can be tagged also as several *types*: POSITION, POSITIONGROUP, INDGROUP, MEMBERGROUP, INDIVIDUAL, MEMBER, PEOPLE and OTHER. Otherwise, within Klue, there are tree different *entities types*: PERSON, PEOPLE, PERSONPEOPLE. As in English the distinction between count and non-count nouns are much more rigid and static than in Portuguese, a system prepared for English must include this distinction in its very first classification. In Portuguese, this feature is more flexible and generally defined only in the syntax level, which is not considered by *entity types* in Klue, since its classification is a context free one. It is interesting to note that this distinction in English is marked at the context free level, which is something impossible for Portuguese.

To make a relation between Klue and HAREM, many *entity types* in Klue were related to *categories*, *category.type* or *category.type.subtypes* tags in HAREM.

Although the objectives of Klue and HAREM are similar – being a tagset to be used to the classification of named entities – what is focused on each typology strategy is very different and it makes the two tagsets very distinct.

Klue has a very clear distinction between the general meaning of a *mention* (represented by *entity types*) and its contextual meaning (*role*). Within Klue, a word must have always the same *entity type* and its *role* can vary depending on the content. HAREM denies the need of having a context free meaning in NER process, since its more basic tag already depends on the context, even in cases of homophones words or expressions.

For example, 'dog' in Klue is always from the *entity type* ANIMAL and can have various *roles*: when used in a generic context, it belongs to the *role* PEOPLE as in 'Dogs are cool'; when used individually, it is tagged as PERSON, e.g. 'My dog is so cool'. Within HAREM, 'dog' in the first sentence in tagged by THING(*category*)/CLASS MEMBER (*type*); and in the last sentence 'dogs' is tagged THING(*category*)/ OBJECT (*type*).

5 Conclusions and future work

We described, in this short paper, an undergoing experiment that aims to compare two different tagsets used to NER. For now, we proposed a comparison table between them and already presented some relevant issues that we have to address before continuing the experiment.

Most issues lie in the different architectures adopted by each tagset, but specific tags which are not really language-independent, as one could expect, are also a challenge. Since Klue is not language specific (and created mainly by English speakers), it has categories which are not so relevant to Portuguese analysis.

Besides the architecture of the two chosen tagsets being different, we compared it focusing on which set of named entities each tag from HAREM included and tried to find the same set in Klue. This methodology seems to be more useful than trying to connect them finding correspondences in the architecture level. We hope that this heuristic solves both kind of problems.

What we still leave to be done is the final part of this experimente which consists in training a model in SIRE with the Golden Collection from HAREM translated to Klue tagset and evaluate the performance of SIRE comparing its results with the tools evaluated in HAREM.

References

Carlos Amaral; Helena Figueira; Afonso Mendes; Pedro Mendes; Claudia Pinto; Amaral. 2008. A workbench for developing natural language processing tools. In *Pre-proceedings of the 1st Workshop on International Proofing Tools and Language Technologies*.

Diana Santos & Nuno Cardoso. 2008a. *Reconhecimento de entidades mencionadas em português: Documentação e actas do HAREM, a primeira avalição conjunta na area*. FCCN, Portugal.

Nuno Cardoso. 2008b. Rembrandt - reconhecimento de entidades mencionadas baseado em relações e análise detalhada do texto. In Cristina Mota; Diana Santos, editor, *Desafios na avaliação conjunta do reconhecimento de entidades mencionadas: O Segundo HAREM*, pages 195–211.

R. Florian, H. Hassan, A. Ittycheriah, H. Jing, N. Kambhatla, X. Luo, N Nicolov, and S Roukos.

2004. A statistical model for multilingual entity detection and tracking. In *Proceedings of HLT-NAACL 2004*, pages 1–8.

Elaine Marsh; Dennis Perzanowski. 1998. Muc-7 evaluation of ie technology: Overview of results. *Muc 7 Proceedings*.

James Pustejovsky. 1995. *The Generative Lexicon*. MIT Press, Cambridge, MA.

Adwait Ratnaparkhi. 1998. *Maximum entropy models for natural language ambiguity resolution*. Ph.D. thesis, University of Pennsylvania.

N. Chinchor; P. Robinson. 1997. Muc-7 named entity task definition. *Message Understanding Conference Proceedings*.

HAREM Category	HAREM Type	HAREM Subtype	Klue Entity Types
person	individual		person
time	calendar	date	date
location	human	discipline	gpe
organization	institution		organization
organization	administration	organization	governamental/mutigov/political
location	human	country	gpe country
person	membergroup	personpeople	
thing	class		**various**
abstraction	discipline		
value	quantity	measure	
location	human	construction	gpe facility
happening	organized		event
work	plan		law
organization	company		organization commercial
person	position		person
work	reproduced		titlework
other			
time	generic		time
happening	ephemeris		event
abstraction	name		
location	human	region	gpe
thing	object		**various**
abstraction	idea		
time	frequency		time
value	currency		money
time	duration		duration
time	timecalend	interval	date
person	people		personpeople
happening	event		event
work	reproduced	book	titlework
work	art		titlework
valor	classification		ordinal
local	physical	region	geologicalobject
time	timecalend	hour	time
person	groupind		personpeople
location	human	street	gpe
location	virtual	site	web
work	reproduced	music	titlework
organization	institution	sub	organization
work	reproduced	movie	titlework
person	groupposition		people
location	physical	watermass	geologicalobject
location	virtual	comsocial	web
work	reproduced	other	titlework
organization			organization
location	human	other	gpe
organization	administration	sub	organization governamental/mutigov/political
happening			event
location			geologicalobject/gpe/web
location	physical	island	geologicalobject
location	physical	other	geologicalobject
location	physical	relief	geologicalobject
abstraction	state		disease
thing	substance		substance
thing	class member		**various**
location	physical	watermass	geologicalobject
location	physical	planet	geologicalobject
location	other		geologicalobject/gpe/web
thing			**various**
person	member		person
abstraction			
work	art	house	titlework
location	virtual	other	web
work			titlework/law
work	art	classification	titlework
location	virtual	work	web
work	reproduced	program	titlework
work	art	other	titlework
person			person
thing	other		**various**
other	other		
location	virtual		web
work	art	painting	titlework
organization	company	sub	organization commercial
work	reproduced	theater	titlework

Table 3: Comparison - HAREM and Klue

Semi-supervised Learning for Vietnamese Named Entity Recognition using Online Conditional Random Fields

Quang H. Pham
University of Science, Vietnam
quangg2012@gmail.com

Minh-Le Nguyen
Japan Advanced Institute of Science and Technology
nguyenml@jaist.ac.jp

Binh T. Nguyen
University of Science, Vietnam
ngtbinh@hcmus.edu.vn

Nguyen Viet Cuong
National University of Singapore
nvcuong@nus.edu.sg

Abstract

We present preliminary results for the named entity recognition problem in the Vietnamese language. For this task, we build a system based on conditional random fields and address one of its challenges: how to combine labeled and unlabeled data to create a stronger system. We propose a set of features that is useful for the task and conduct experiments with different settings to show that using bootstrapping with an online learning algorithm called Margin Infused Relaxed Algorithm increases the performance of the models.

1 Introduction

Named Entity Recognition (NER) is an important problem in natural language processing and has been investigated for many years (Tjong Kim Sang and De Meulder, 2003). There have been a lot of works on this task, especially for major languages such as English, Chinese, etc. (McCallum and Li, 2003; Gao et al., 2005; Ritter et al., 2011). For the Vietnamese language, several authors have attempted to tackle the NER problem using both supervised and semi-supervised methods (Tu et al., 2005; Tran et al., 2007; Nguyen et al., 2010; Pham et al., 2012; Le Trung et al., 2014). However, previous works for NER in the Vietnamese language mainly used offline supervised learning methods, where all the training data are gathered before a model is trained.

In this paper, we report preliminary results for a Vietnamese NER system trained by using conditional random fields (CRFs) (Lafferty et al., 2001). Unlike previous works for NER in the Vietnamese language, we use an online learning algorithm, the Margin Infused Relaxed Algorithm (MIRA) (Crammer and Singer, 2003), to train the CRFs. Furthermore, due to the fact that the number of labeled data is small while that of unlabeled data is very large, we treat this problem under the semi-supervised learning framework. In particular, we use the bootstrapping method on top of the CRF models to gradually increase the number of labeled data. Using bootstrapping, a small number of new labeled training data are available after each round and then can be used to update the CRF model.

We demonstrate that using MIRA to learn CRFs instead of the traditional offline method would increase the performance of our system. We also propose a set of features that is useful for this task and gives competitive performance. In contrast to previous works such as (Tran et al., 2007), we do not use features from outside sources, e.g. gazetteer features; so our feature set does not require human effort to create such resources and therefore, is easy to build.

The rest of this paper is organized as follows. In Section 2, we review some previous works for the NER task, especially for the Vietnamese language. A brief introduction to CRF and MIRA is given in Section 3. This will be followed by a description of our feature set in Section 4. In Section 5, we describe our semi-supervised learning approach for the Vietnamese NER problem. We show our experimental setup and results in Section 6. In Section 7, we give some discussions about the problem. Finally, we conclude our paper and discuss some future works in Section 8.

2 Related Works

NER is an important problem that was first introduced at the Sixth Message Understanding Conference (MUC–6) (Grishman and Sundheim, 1996)

Proceedings of the Fifth Named Entity Workshop, joint with 53rd ACL and the 7th IJCNLP, pages 50–55,
Beijing, China, July 26-31, 2015. ©2015 Association for Computational Linguistics

and since then has attracted many researchers to investigate the problem with new methods as well as different languages. Over the years, researchers have tried to solve the problem under supervised learning (McCallum and Li, 2003), semi-supervised learning (Ji and Grishman, 2006), and unsupervised learning (Etzioni et al., 2005) frameworks. One dominant approach for NER is supervised learning with conditional random fields (McCallum and Li, 2003). However, semi-supervised learning approaches are also attractive for this task because it is expensive to get a large amount of labeled data. Notably, Riloff et al. (1999) introduced the mutual bootstrapping method that proved to be highly influential. Besides, using bootstrapping methods, Ji and Grishman (2006) were able to improve the performance of existing NER systems.

For the Vietnamese language, using supervised learning, Tu et al. (2005) built an NER system with CRFs and reported 87.90% F_1 score as their highest performance. Using SVMs, Tran et al. (2007) achieved 87.75% F_1 score for the task. For semi-supervised learning, Pham et al. (2012) achieved 90.14% F_1 score using CRFs with the generalized expectation criteria (Mann and McCallum, 2010), while Le Trung et al. (2014) reported an accuracy of 95% for their system that uses bootstrapping and rule-based models.

3 Margin Infused Relaxed Algorithm for CRFs

3.1 Conditional Random Fields

Linear-chain conditional random field (CRF) is a sequence labeling model first introduced by Lafferty et al. (2001). This model allows us to define a rich set of features to capture complex dependencies between a structured observation $\mathbf{x}$ and its corresponding structured label $\mathbf{y}$. Throughout this paper, we will use the term CRF to refer to linear-chain CRF, a widely used type of CRFs in which $\mathbf{x}$ and $\mathbf{y}$ have linear-chain structures.

Formally, let $\mathbf{x} = (x_1, x_2, \ldots, x_T)$ be the input sequence, $\mathbf{y} = (y_1, y_2, \ldots, y_T)$ be the label sequence, $\mathcal{F} = \{f_k(y_t, y_{t-1}, \mathbf{x})\}_{k=1}^K$ be a set of real-valued functions (features) over two consecutive labels y_t, y_{t-1} and the input sequence $\mathbf{x}$, and $\Lambda = \{\lambda_k\}_{k=1}^K$ be the set of parameters associated with the features that we want to learn. A linear-chain CRF defines the conditional distribution $p(\mathbf{y}|\mathbf{x})$ as:

$$p(\mathbf{y}|\mathbf{x}) = \frac{1}{Z(\mathbf{x})} \exp\left(\sum_{k=1}^{K}\sum_{t=1}^{T} \lambda_k f_k(y_t, y_{t-1}, \mathbf{x})\right)$$

where $Z(\mathbf{x}) = \sum_{\mathbf{y}} \exp\left(\sum_{k=1}^{K}\sum_{t=1}^{T} \lambda_k f_k(y_t, y_{t-1}, \mathbf{x})\right)$ is the normalization constant, also called the partition function.

Normally, training a CRF is an iterative process where all the parameters are updated after each iteration to maximize the conditional log-likelihood of the training data. During testing, the label sequence for a new test instance is determined by a Viterbi-like algorithm, which returns the label sequence with the highest probability according to the trained model (Sutton and McCallum, 2006).

3.2 Margin Infused Relaxed Algorithm

MIRA is an online learning algorithm developed by Crammer and Singer (2003). In this algorithm, at each round, the model receives a training example, makes a prediction on the example, and suffers a loss. Then the training algorithm updates the weight vector so that the norm of the change to the weight vector is as small as possible while keeping a margin at least as large as the loss of the incorrect examples.

Details of the single-best MIRA (Crammer, 2004; McDonald et al., 2005) for the sequence labeling task are given in Algorithm 1. In the update step at line 4 of the algorithm, $s(\mathbf{x}, \mathbf{y})$ is a scoring function and $L(\mathbf{y}, \mathbf{y}')$ is a loss function. The difference between MIRA and offline training for CRFs is that MIRA processes one data example at a time while the offline algorithm processes all the data at each iteration. However, the features and the prediction algorithm are identical regardless of the learning algorithms.

4 Features for CRFs

We model NER as a sequence labeling task where each word in a sentence is associated with a tag to indicate which type of named entities it belongs to. There are 5 possible tags that we are interested in: *person*, *organization*, *location*, *miscellaneous* (proper names), and *none*. The *none* tag indicates that the corresponding word is not a part of any named entity. For instance, it may be a verb or an adjective.

We build a set of features that is useful for the Vietnamese NER task. Recall that a feature

Algorithm 1 MIRA for Sequence Labeling

INPUT: Training data $\mathcal{D} = \{(\mathbf{x}_t, \mathbf{y}_t)\}_{t=1}^{|\mathcal{D}|}$, number of iterations N.

$\mathbf{w}_0 \leftarrow \mathbf{0}$; $\mathbf{v} \leftarrow \mathbf{0}$; $i = 0$;
for $n = 1$ to N **do**
  for $t = 1$ to $|\mathcal{D}|$ **do**
    $\mathbf{w}_{i+1} \leftarrow \arg\min_{\mathbf{w}} \|\mathbf{w} - \mathbf{w}_i\|$ such that $s(\mathbf{x}_t, \mathbf{y}_t) - s(\mathbf{x}_t, \mathbf{y}) \geq L(\mathbf{y}_t, \mathbf{y}), \forall \mathbf{y}$;
    $\mathbf{v} \leftarrow \mathbf{v} + \mathbf{w}_{i+1}$;
    $i \leftarrow i + 1$;
  end for
end for
return $\mathbf{v}/(N \times T)$;

in CRFs is a function over the observation $\mathbf{x}$ and two consecutive labels y_t and y_{t-1}. In this paper, we use as features the binary functions that can be fully defined based on the observation sequence.

Particularly, the first type of features we use is the identity of words in a window of size 5 and their combinations. Besides, information about capitalization plays a notably important role for this task. For example, a person's name always has its first letter capitalized, and an abbreviation of a company's name or a place is all capitalized (e.g. Ho Chi Minh city is abbreviated as HCM). Thus, we add orthographic features to feed this information into the CRFs. This type of features describes whether a word is in lower case, whether it has the first letter capitalized, whether all of its letters are capitalized, and whether it contains numeric letters or not. For this type of features, we also take the orthographic information of words in a window of size 5. Finally, we include as features the part-of-speech of the word and the combination of the word's identity and its part-of-speech to better describe the context of the sentence.

We note that not all of the features described above are used since there are possibly redundant features that do not increase the performance. Therefore, we conduct a feature selection step for choosing which features to be utilized for later experiments. We first start with the current word's identity and orthographic features. Then, we add several features, build an appropriate model, and measure its performance on a validation set, which contains 150 sentences extracted from the total training data. If the performance increases, we keep those features; otherwise, they are discarded. The process of adding and discarding features is repeated until there is no more feature left to be added.

Group	Features
Single	W_0, W_{-1}, W_1, W_{-2}, W_2, $W_{-1,0}$, $W_{0,1}$, $W_{-2,-1}$, $W_{1,2}$, $W_{-1,0,1}$, $W_{-2,-1,0}$, $W_{0,1,2}$, , O_0 , P_{-1}, P_0, P_1, $P_{-1,0}$, $P_{0,1}$, $P_{-2,-1}$, $P_{1,2}$
Complex	W_0P_1, $W_0P_0O_0$, W_0O_0, $W_0W_{-1}O_0O_{-1}$, $W_0W_1O_0O_1$

Table 1: Features for training the CRFs. The subscripts indicate the position of the features relatively to the current position.

In Table 1, we give the final set of our features. This set includes 2 groups: single and complex features. The first group contains features about word identity (W), part-of-speech (P), and orthographic information (O). Complex features are formed by combining the single features. From Table 1, possible word identity features such as $W_{-1,1}$ and $W_{-2,2}$ are not listed because they were eliminated during the feature selection step.

5 Bootstrapping with CRFs

One main difficulty of the Vietnamese NER task is the lack of labeled data. Since texts from news, books, etc. naturally do not come with named entity labels, we have to manually label the data set. This is tedious and time consuming when the data size becomes very large. One way to address this problem is to gradually create more labeled data with just a small amount of labeled data via semi-supervised learning.

More specifically, we use the bootstrapping method in this paper. First, we build a model on a labeled corpus and use it to label the data from a data set that has not been labeled. After that, we select some newly labeled instances (sentences in our case), remove them from the unlabeled data set, and add them to the labeled data set. The criteria for choosing instances may vary and depend on the task. Then, the next model is trained on the new labeled set and it will also get an amount of new labeled data from the unlabeled data set. This process is repeated until we satisfy with the amount of labeled data that have been received.

We provide our CRF training procedure with bootstrapping in Algorithm 2. The criterion for choosing the sentences from the unlabeled data

Algorithm 2 Bootstrapping with CRFs

INPUT: Labeled data set L, unlabeled data set U, number of iterations n, the amount of sentences per round k.

for $i = 0$ to n **do**
  Train CRF model M_i on data set L.
  Use M_i to label U.
  Choose k labeled sentences $X = \{\mathbf{x}_j\}_{j=1}^{k}$ with highest confidence from U.
  $L \leftarrow L \cup X; \quad U \leftarrow U \setminus X.$
end for
return M_n.

set is to choose the sentence whose best label sequence got the highest probability assigned by the model.

6 Experimental Results

6.1 Setup

We build a corpus of 1,911 sentences from law news articles and manually tag their named entity labels. To build the unlabeled data set, we collect another 17,500 sentences, which also come from law articles .Both data sets are collected from online newspaper articles. The labeled data set is annotated using the IBO label format (Tjong Kim Sang and De Meulder, 2003) with the 5 labels mentioned in Section 4.

For the bootstrapping experiments, we split our corpus into two parts: the first part contains a fixed set of 411 sentences for testing, and the second part contains 1500 sentences for training. We train 3 initial models using 500, 1000, and 1500 sentences respectively from the second part and apply the bootstrapping algorithm to each trained model, with the maximum number of iterations n being 15. In each iteration, the model selects the top $k = 10$ highest confidence (i.e., highest value of $p(\mathbf{y}|\mathbf{x}, \Lambda)$) sentences to add into its training set. Finally, we compare the results of these models after 5, 10, and 15 rounds of bootstrapping with the initial models. To evaluate the performance of the models, we use the micro-averaged precision (P), recall (R), and F_1 score (F).

In our experiments, we use the CRF++ toolkit[1] which comes with MIRA training option to build our models. Regarding the tasks of Vietnamese word segmentation and part-of-speech tagging, we use a standard tool for Vietnamese language processing provided by Nguyen et al. (2005).

[1]The toolkit is available at: `http://taku910.github.io/crfpp`.

6.2 Results

In Table 2, we depict the highest F_1 score (in %) of the models for every 5 rounds of bootstrapping. For all the initial training sizes, the best CRF trained using MIRA outperforms the best normal CRF in the semi-supervised learning scenario. With 1000 initial training sentences, we achieve the highest increase in F_1 score (which is 2.43%) after 5 rounds of bootstrapping with MIRA compared to not using bootstrapping. Our highest performance is 89.16%, obtained by training with 1500 initial sentences and after 15 rounds of bootstrapping with MIRA.

It is interesting to note that the performance does not always increase after every round. From our error analysis, whenever a model makes a mistake at a round, it affects all the following models and makes them more inaccurate. This leads to a decrease of F_1 score for the later models on the fixed test set.

7 Discussions

When inspecting the best model in Table 2 (CRF model using MIRA with 1500 training sentences and 10 rounds of bootstrapping), we find several cases that may be difficult for the model to predict. In the examples below, every two consecutive words are separated by a white space, the syllables in each word are connected by underscores, and the bold phrases include one word and its wrongly predicted label. All words having the *none* label or having been correctly classified are neither in bold nor followed by any label.

For the Vietnamese language, we find that the model may easily confuse a person name with a location name and vice versa. For instance, the model may mistake a person name for a location name as in the following sentence:

> Họ nói rằng lượng hàng hoá họ nhận được có nguồn từ **Trần_Thế_Luân/location**.
>
> (They said that all the goods they received originated from Tran_The_Luan.)

Here, the word "Trần_Thế_Luân" refers to a person name rather than a location name as predicted above. In this case, the confusion may be caused

#Data	CRF with MIRA				Normal (offline) CRF			
	0	5	10	15	0	5	10	15
500	84.78	**85.69**	83.73	84.60	83.24	83.22	82.93	82.90
1000	85.91	**88.34**	87.11	87.11	87.67	87.59	87.67	87.14
1500	88.12	88.15	**89.16**	87.96	88.58	88.70	88.74	88.16

Table 2: Results of bootstrapping with different initial training sizes after 0, 5, 10, and 15 rounds of bootstrapping. The bold figures are the best F_1 scores with respect to a training size.

by the similar sentence structures when using a person name or a location name. For example, we can replace the word "Trần_Thế_Luân" in the sentence above by a location name and the sentence is still correct. Furthermore, in Vietnamese, many person names are used to name the locations. This also makes it more difficult to distinguish these two labels.

Another source of mistakes is the confusion between an organization name and a person name. For example, the following sentence was added during bootstrapping:

> Trong_khi_đó, **ACB/none** đang dư tiền nên đã chuyển cho **Vietbank/person** và **Kienlongbank/person**.
>
> (In the meantime, ACB is having a lot of extra money, so they transfer some to both Vietbank and Kienlongbank.)

In this example, the model could not recognize "ACB" as an organization name, and it also misclassified "Vietbank" and "Kienlongbank" as person names (ACB, Vietbank, and Kienlongbank are in fact three major banks in Vietnam). This is a difficult case since the English word "bank" is concatenated with the word "Viet" and "Kienlong", and thus it is harder to classify these words without using an external dictionary. Moreover, the sentence structure also cannot help to distinguish the two labels in this case because we can replace the three words "ACB", "Vietbank", and "Kienlongbank" by three person names and the sentence is still correct.

8 Conclusions and Future Works

We have presented preliminary results for a Vietnamese NER system trained using the CRF with MIRA and bootstrapping. We also proposed a set of useful features, which are easy to compute and do not need human work for processing unlabeled data. Our experiments showed that combining CRFs trained by MIRA with bootstrapping increases our system's performance.

For future works, we will focus on how to choose more meaningful sentences from the unlabeled data set and how to enhance the bootstrapping algorithm for the NER task. Since there are many algorithms to build our model, investigating how to combine these models in the semi-supervised learning framework to achieve better results is also a promising direction.

Acknowledgments

This work was carried out when the first author participated in an internship program at the Japan Advanced Institute of Science and Technology.

References

Koby Crammer and Yoram Singer. 2003. Ultraconservative online algorithms for multiclass problems. *Journal of Machine Learning Research*, 3:951–991.

Yacov Shlomo Crammer. 2004. *Online learning of complex categorical problems*. Ph.D. thesis, Hebrew University of Jerusalem.

Oren Etzioni, Michael Cafarella, Doug Downey, Ana-Maria Popescu, Tal Shaked, Stephen Soderland, Daniel S. Weld, and Alexander Yates. 2005. Unsupervised named-entity extraction from the web: An experimental study. *Artificial intelligence*, 165(1):91–134.

Jianfeng Gao, Mu Li, Andi Wu, and Chang-Ning Huang. 2005. Chinese word segmentation and named entity recognition: A pragmatic approach. *Computational Linguistics*, 31(4):531–574.

Ralph Grishman and Beth Sundheim. 1996. Message Understanding Conference-6: A Brief History. In *International Conference on Computational Linguistics (COLING)*, volume 96, pages 466–471.

Heng Ji and Ralph Grishman. 2006. Data selection in semi-supervised learning for name tagging. In *Workshop on Information Extraction Beyond The Document*, pages 48–55.

John Lafferty, Andrew McCallum, and Fernando C.N. Pereira. 2001. Conditional random fields: Probabilistic models for segmenting and labeling sequence data. In *International Conference on Machine Learning (ICML)*.

Hieu Le Trung, Vu Le Anh, and Kien Le Trung. 2014. Bootstrapping and rule-based model for recognizing Vietnamese named entity. In *Asian Conference on Intelligent Information and Database Systems (ACIIDS)*, pages 167–176.

Gideon S. Mann and Andrew McCallum. 2010. Generalized expectation criteria for semi-supervised learning with weakly labeled data. *Jounral of Machine Learning Research*, 11:955–984.

Andrew McCallum and Wei Li. 2003. Early results for named entity recognition with conditional random fields, feature induction and web-enhanced lexicons. In *Conference on Natural Language Learning at HLT-NAACL (CoNLL)*, pages 188–191.

Ryan McDonald, Koby Crammer, and Fernando Pereira. 2005. Online large-margin training of dependency parsers. In *Annual Meeting of the Association for Computational Linguistics (ACL)*, pages 91–98.

Cam-Tu Nguyen, Xuan-Hieu Phan, and Thu-Trang Nguyen. 2005. JVnTextPro: A tool to process Vietnamese texts.

Dat Ba Nguyen, Son Huu Hoang, Son Bao Pham, and Thai Phuong Nguyen. 2010. Named entity recognition for Vietnamese. In *Asian Conference on Intelligent Information and Database Systems (ACIIDS)*, pages 205–214.

Thi-Ngan Pham, Le Minh Nguyen, and Quang-Thuy Ha. 2012. Named entity recognition for Vietnamese documents using semi-supervised learning method of CRFs with generalized expectation criteria. In *International Conference on Asian Language Processing (IALP)*, pages 85–88.

Ellen Riloff, Rosie Jones, et al. 1999. Learning dictionaries for information extraction by multi-level bootstrapping. In *AAAI Conference on Artificial Intelligence*, pages 474–479.

Alan Ritter, Sam Clark, Oren Etzioni, et al. 2011. Named entity recognition in tweets: an experimental study. In *Conference on Empirical Methods in Natural Language Processing (EMNLP)*, pages 1524–1534.

Charles Sutton and Andrew McCallum. 2006. An introduction to conditional random fields for relational learning. *Introduction to Statistical Relational Learning*, pages 93–128.

Erik F. Tjong Kim Sang and Fien De Meulder. 2003. Introduction to the CoNLL-2003 shared task: Language-independent named entity recognition. In *Conference on Natural Language Learning at HLT-NAACL (CoNLL)*, pages 142–147.

Q. Tri Tran, T.X. Thao Pham, Q. Hung Ngo, Dien Dinh, and Nigel Collier. 2007. Named entity recognition in Vietnamese documents. *Progress in Informatics*, 5:14–17.

Nguyen Cam Tu, Tran Thi Oanh, Phan Xuan Hieu, and Ha Quang Thuy. 2005. Named entity recognition in Vietnamese free-text and web documents using conditional random fields. In *Conference on Some Selection Problems of Information Technology and Telecommunication*.

Boosting English-Chinese Machine Transliteration via High Quality Alignment and Multilingual Resources

Yan Shao, Jörg Tiedemann, Joakim Nivre
Department of Linguistics and Philology
Uppsala University
{yan.shao, jorg.tiedemann, joakim.nivre}@lingfil.uu.se

Abstract

This paper presents our machine transliteration systems developed for the NEWS 2015 machine transliteration shared task. Our systems are applied to two tasks: English to Chinese and Chinese to English. For standard runs, in which only official data sets are used, we build phrase-based transliteration models with refined alignments provided by the M2M-aligner. For non-standard runs, we add multilingual resources to the systems designed for the standard runs and build different language specific transliteration systems. Linear regression is adopted to rerank the outputs afterwards, which significantly improves the overall transliteration performance.

1 Introduction

Machine transliteration is an effective approach to process named entities that are out-of-vocabulary words in many NLP tasks, such as machine translation, corpus alignment and cross-language information retrieval. In this paper, using the experiment data from the NEWS 2015 machine transliteration shared task (Zhang et al., 2015), we develop machine transliteration systems respectively targeting English to Chinese and Chinese to English transliteration tasks.

The M2M-aligner (Jiampojamarn et al., 2007) is used to preprocess the training data to obtain the boundaries and alignments of transliteration units between source and target language. We apply a hard-constrained estimation-maximization (EM) algorithm to post-process its outputs, which greatly reduces errors of segmentation and alignment. With the refined outputs, we build phrase-based transliteration systems using Moses (Koehn et al., 2007), a popular statistical machine translation framework. The results are submitted as standard runs.

Since transliteration is the transcription preserving the pronunciation of the source language, source names that are written in the same script can be pronounced differently in different language and therefore the transliterations will not be the same. Thus, we build various language specific transliteration systems using multilingual resources. Linear regression is used to rerank the outputs, where the individual scores of translation models in Moses are used as features. The results are submitted as non-standard runs.

2 Background

Machine transliteration is often modelled as a sequence labelling problem in previous research. Thus, the existing algorithms for sequence labelling all can be used for solving the problem. The classical joint source-channel model (Li et al., 2004) is essentially a Hidden Markov Model (HMM), which allows direct mapping between the transliteration units in source and target languages. Given the source string as the input, when it passes through the joint source-channel, the output is generated simultaneously.

Chen et al. (2011) extends the original source-channel model into multi-to-multi source-channel model and uses Moses as the decoder. As a popular experimental framework for machine translation, Moses is also applied to build phrase-based transliteration systems in some other related works (Finch and Sumita, 2010). Machine transliteration is treated as character level machine translation without distortion in their approaches.

In addition, the use of Conditional Random Fields (CRF) (Lafferty et al., 2001) is another popular approach in previous studies. It is a powerful discriminative sequence labelling model that uses rich local features. However, it is very costly in terms of time complexity during the training process especially combined with the full transliteration task. Qin and Chen (2011) decomposes the

Proceedings of the Fifth Named Entity Workshop, joint with 53rd ACL and the 7th IJCNLP, pages 56–60,
Beijing, China, July 26-31, 2015. ©2015 Association for Computational Linguistics

full task into several subtasks and uses different CRF recognizers. Kuo et al. (2012) uses a two-stage CRF system with accessor variety (AV) as an additional feature, which processes segmentation and mapping separately.

3 System Description

3.1 Preprocessing Training Data

As in the case of machine translation, the training data for constructing transliteration systems usually do not contain required alignments between source and target languages. In this study, we use the M2M-Aligner to preprocess the training data and obtain the boundaries and alignment information of transliteration units. The M2M-Aligner uses an EM algorithm, which is an extension of the forward-backward training of the one-to-one stochastic transducer originally presented by Ristad and Yianilos (1998).

Since the performance of the aligner has a great impact on the overall transliteration quality, we preprocess the M2M-Aligner's input as well as post-process its output to retrieve better segmentations and alignments. The basic units in English and Chinese are respectively single letters and single Chinese characters in the M2M-Aligner's input. For English, some letter combinations, namely *ch, ck, sh* and two identical letters appearing next to each other are always pronounced as single letters and hence never aligned to different Chinese characters. We pre-contract them so that the M2M-Aligner will treat them as single letters and never segment those combinations incorrectly.

Due to the fact that single Chinese characters are normally independent transliteration units, in most cases several English letters are aligned to one Chinese character. The letter x is the only exception as it may be aligned to two Chinese characters, which will be handled by post-processing in this paper. Despite of that, we set the maximum length of substring on the English side as six and on the Chinese side as one. All the other parameters of the M2M-Aligner have default settings.

Table 1 shows an output sample. In order to reduce the segmentation and alignment errors further, we first modify the alignments associated with x and then post-process the output using a hard-constrained EM algorithm.

It is easy to find from the training data that when the letter x should be mapped to two neighboring characters A and B, A's corresponding pinyin is always *ke* and B's pinyin always starts with *s* or *x*. With the help of pinyin, it is straightforward to extract all the instances in which x should be aligned to two Chinese characters but have been incorrectly processed by the M2M-Aligner. For those instances, we erase the boundaries between the two Chinese characters A, B which x is aligned to. On the English side, we remove the boundary closest to x. After the modification, the third and fourth instances in Table 1 will be changed as the ones in Table 2. The segmentations and alignments are still not correct but it is now possible to continue with the next stage.

a|ber|nat|hy|	阿|伯|内|西|
a|ber|ne|thy|	阿|伯|内|西|
t|e|xi|do|	特|克|西|多|
wi|ll|c|o|x|	威|尔|科|克|斯|

Table 1: Sample output of M2M Aligner

t|exi|do|	特|克西|多|
wi|ll|c|ox|	威|尔|科|克斯|

Table 2: Sample segmentations and alignments

We assume that the segmentations and alignments with low frequencies are very likely to be errors produces by the M2M-Aligner. In this respect, we develop an algorithm which largely reduces the low frequency terms and therefore significantly improves the segmentation and alignment quality. Given the current output, we estimate the probability of an individual instance s by:

$$p(s) = \prod_{i=1}^{n} p(e_i)p(e_i \leftrightarrow c_i) \tag{1}$$

where $p(e_i)$ is the probability of segmented substring e_i on the English side and $p(e_i \leftrightarrow c_i)$ is the probability of e_i aligned to c_i, which is on the Chinese side. Using maximum likelihood estimation (MLE), $p(e_i)$ and $p(e_i \leftrightarrow c_i)$ are calculated as:

$$p(e_i) = \frac{c(e_i) + 1}{N + R} \tag{2}$$

$$p(e_i \leftrightarrow c_i) = \frac{c(e_i \leftrightarrow c_i) + 1}{N + R} \tag{3}$$

N is the total number of segmented substrings or alignments. R is the number of unique substrings, which works as a smoothing factor. $c(e_i)$ and

$c(e_i \leftrightarrow c_i)$ are respectively the counts of the substring e_i and corresponding alignment.

We use the obtained probabilities to reassess and modify the current segmentations and alignments. To maximize the probability presented in formula 1, a local greedy search strategy is used for efficiency. For every two neighboring substrings on the English side, we find the best split point as their new boundary. The probabilities are updated afterwards. This procedure iterates until it converges. Table 3 shows the segmentation and alignment results after the EM post-processing. According to error inspection, the refined result is significantly better than the original one even though there are still mistakes involved.

<table>
<tr><td>a|ber|na|thy|</td><td>阿|伯|内|西|</td></tr>
<tr><td>a|ber|ne|thy|</td><td>阿|伯|内|西|</td></tr>
<tr><td>t|exi|do|</td><td>特|克西|多|</td></tr>
<tr><td>wi|ll|co|x|</td><td>威|尔|科|克斯|</td></tr>
</table>

Table 3: Sample segmentations and alignments

3.2 Phrase-Based Machine Transliteration

In this paper, we build our phrase-based transliteration systems with Moses using the refined outputs of the M2M-Aligner. The output can be easily converted into the format of alignment files that are generated by Moses after its third training step. We build the system from step four with default parameters. We use IRSTLM (Federico et al., 2008) to build language models with order 6.

For English to Chinese transliteration, we build two systems with different transliteration units on the English side. First, we build a full character based system, in which all the single letters are basic mapping units. At the decoding stage, the source English names can be input directly as strings of letters and the Moses decoder will identify the phrase boundaries and map the phrases as transliteration units to target Chinese characters.

Additionally, we build a system with pre-segmented substrings on the English side as basic units. In this case, at the decoding stage, pre-segmenting the source English names is required. A CRF segmentation model is trained using the CRF++ toolkit. However, since the CRF model essentially does the segmentation via identifying the boundaries, some produced substrings are not known to the transliteration model. They are treated as OOVs and therefore will not be transliterated. Under these circumstances, we combine the two systems. When the input cannot be transliterated by the system built with pre-segmented substrings, the output of the character based system is used as backoff.

For Chinese to English transliteration, we build two character based systems. The first one is trained with Chinese characters and the second one with corresponding Chinese pinyin. The pinyin based system is used similarly as backoff because occasionally there are some uncommon Chinese characters that are not seen in the training data. However, there are always Chinese characters contained in the training data that share the same pronunciations as the unknown ones. They also have the same pinyin as it is the phonetic representation of Chinese character.

All the systems are tuned with the official development data sets.

3.3 Using Multilingual Resources

Transliteration is based on phonetics and therefore it is heavily language dependent. The western names associated with transliteration tasks are written in the same script but actually have different language origins. Thus, they should be transliterated using different language specific systems.

We use the dictionary *Chinese Transliteration of Foreign Personal Names* (Xia, 1993) as our bilingual resources, which is also used in Li et al. (2004)'s research. It contains western names from different language origins and their Chinese transliterations. In this research, we choose the western language sources that have more than 10,000 terms in the dictionary to build backoff transliteration systems introduced in the previous section. The chosen languages are Czech, English, Finnish, French, Turkish, German, Portuguese, Hungarian, Italian, Romanian, Russian, Spanish, Swedish and Serbian.

For the English to Chinese development set, 1,783 instances out of 2,802 are found in the dictionary. Among them, 1,645 have at least one correct transliteration in the dictionary while 318 have at least one correct transliteration that is not in the dictionary. The statistics is similar for the Chinese to English development set.

For the test data, we apply the source name to all the language specific systems. For each term, every system returns 10 different scores of Moses, such as total score, language model score, phrase

		Standard Runs					Non-Standard Runs				
Tasks	Test Sets	Configuration	ACC	F-score	MRR	MAP_{ref}	Configuration	ACC	F-score	MRR	MAP_{ref}
EnCh	NEWS11	Character Based	0.324	0.682	0.404	0.312	Baseline	0.365	0.708	0.431	0.351
		Subtring Based	0.333	0.673	0.387	0.320	Reranking	0.722	0.870	0.775	0.717
		Backoff System	0.340	0.694	0.397	0.327					
	NEWS12	Character Based	0.311	0.660	0.396	0.303	Baseline	0.373	0.693	0.436	0.363
		Subtring Based	0.325	0.660	0.384	0.313	Reranking	0.656	0.824	0.735	0.649
		Backoff System	0.335	0.676	0.396	0.323					
ChEn	NEWS11	Character Based	0.150	0.755	0.228	0.150	Baseline	0.165	0.773	0.252	0.164
		Pinyin Based	0.109	0.731	0.183	0.109	Reranking	0.354	0.833	0.428	0.354
		Backoff System	0.153	0.768	0.233	0.153					
	NEWS12	Character Based	0.191	0.711	0.271	0.187	Baseline	0.214	0.745	0.305	0.212
		Pinyin Based	0.146	0.712	0.223	0.143	Reranking	0.345	0.805	0.421	0.345
		Backoff System	0.199	0.752	0.280	0.194					

Table 4: Official Results

score and different translation model scores. They can be used as features for reranking these outputs by different systems. With respect to the mean F-score, we train a linear regression model using WEKA (Hall et al., 2009) on the development data sets and use it as the reranking system. Additionally, the baseline systems are trained only using the English data from the dictionary to be compared with the multilingual reranking model.

4 Experimental Results and Analysis

Table 4 shows the official experimental results.

4.1 Standard Runs

Since the test data sets are the same as the ones used in the NEWS transliteration shared tasks of 2011 and 2012, our systems are compared to the evaluated systems in the previous years.

For English to Chinese, our system beats all the systems of 2012 (Zhang et al., 2012) but fails to beat the best performing system of 2011 (Zhang et al., 2011) according to ACC. Generally, the substring based system achieves better results than the character based system, which indicates that the CRF model is more effective in identifying phrase boundaries than Moses.

For Chinese to English, our system is slightly worse than the best performing systems but still very competitive. We can see that the Chinese character based system yields better results. Compared to pinyin, Chinese characters contain more information that is useful to transliteration.

As expected, the backoff systems perform best in both tasks. It is also notable that our systems perform better on NEWS12 test data sets, probably because the NEWS12 test data are more similar to the development sets that are used for tuning.

4.2 Non-Standard Runs

For both tasks, our multilingual reranking models significantly outperform the baseline systems. We saw earlier that the dictionary used for training covers a substantial part of the development sets and we assume it is similar for the test sets. Nevertheless, adding multilingual resources leads machine transliteration quality to a new level.

Transliteration without language source discrimination is very difficult because the phonetic systems of different languages are very inconsistent. Take an instance from the development data, *Arbos* as a Spanish name is transliterated as 阿沃斯 in Chinese. If using the transliteration system trained with English names, it is almost impossible to obtain the correct transliteration because *b* is never pronounced as *v* in English.

Our multilingual reranking model can be improved further via adding more multilingual resources, using more effective features for reranking and adopting better regression algorithms.

5 Conclusions

We build phrase based transliteration systems using Moses with refined alignments of the M2M-Aligner. The evaluation results of the standard runs indicate that our approaches are effective in solving both English to Chinese and Chinese to English transliteration tasks. The results of the non-standard runs demonstrate that the transliteration quality can be greatly improved using multilingual resources and good reranking techniques.

References

Yu Chen, Rui Wang, and Yi Zhang. 2011. Statistical machine transliteration with multi-to-multi joint source channel model. In *Proceedings of the Named Entities Workshop Shared Task on Machine Transliteration*, Chiang Mai, Thailand.

Marcello Federico, Nicola Bertoldi, and Mauro Cettolo. 2008. Irstlm: an open source toolkit for handling large scale language models. In *INTERSPEECH*, pages 1618–1621. ISCA.

Andrew Finch and Eiichiro Sumita. 2010. Transliteration using a phrase-based statistical machine translation system to re-score the output of a joint multigram model. In *Proceedings of the 2010 Named Entities Workshop*, NEWS '10, pages 48–52, Stroudsburg, PA, USA. Association for Computational Linguistics.

Mark Hall, Eibe Frank, Geoffrey Holmes, Bernhard Pfahringer, Peter Reutemann, and Ian H. Witten. 2009. The weka data mining software: An update. *SIGKDD Explor. Newsl.*, 11(1):10–18, November.

Sittichai Jiampojamarn, Grzegorz Kondrak, and Tarek Sherif. 2007. Applying many-to-many alignments and hidden markov models to letter-to-phoneme conversion. In *Human Language Technologies 2007: The Conference of the North American Chapter of the Association for Computational Linguistics; Proceedings of the Main Conference*, pages 372–379, Rochester, New York, April. Association for Computational Linguistics.

Philipp Koehn, Hieu Hoang, Alexandra Birch, Chris Callison-Burch, Marcello Federico, Nicola Bertoldi, Brooke Cowan, Wade Shen, Christine Moran, Richard Zens, Chris Dyer, Ondřej Bojar, Alexandra Constantin, and Evan Herbst. 2007. Moses: Open source toolkit for statistical machine translation. In *Proceedings of the 45th Annual Meeting of the ACL on Interactive Poster and Demonstration Sessions*, ACL '07, pages 177–180, Stroudsburg, PA, USA. Association for Computational Linguistics.

Chan-Hung Kuo, Shih-Hung Liu, Tian-Jian Mike Jiang, Cheng-Wei Lee, and Wen-Lian Hsu, 2012. *Proceedings of the 4th Named Entity Workshop (NEWS) 2012*, chapter Cost-benefit Analysis of Two-Stage Conditional Random Fields based English-to-Chinese Machine Transliteration, pages 76–80. Association for Computational Linguistics.

John D. Lafferty, Andrew McCallum, and Fernando C. N. Pereira. 2001. Conditional random fields: Probabilistic models for segmenting and labeling sequence data. In *Proceedings of the Eighteenth International Conference on Machine Learning*, ICML '01, pages 282–289, San Francisco, CA, USA. Morgan Kaufmann Publishers Inc.

Haizhou Li, Min Zhang, and Jian Su. 2004. A joint source-channel model for machine transliteration. In *Proceedings of the 42Nd Annual Meeting on Association for Computational Linguistics*, ACL '04, Stroudsburg, PA, USA. Association for Computational Linguistics.

Ying Qin and GuoHua Chen, 2011. *Proceedings of the 3rd Named Entities Workshop (NEWS 2011)*, chapter Forward-backward Machine Transliteration between English and Chinese Based on Combined CRFs, pages 82–85. Asian Federation of Natural Language Processing.

Eric Sven Ristad and Peter N. Yianilos. 1998. Learning string edit distance. *IEEE Transactions on Pattern Recognition and Machine Intelligence*, 20(5):522–532, May.

Defu Xia. 1993. *Translation Dictionary for Foreign Names*. China Translation and Publishing Corporation, Beijing, China, October.

Min Zhang, Haizhou Li, A. Kumaran, and Ming Liu. 2011. Report of news 2011 machine transliteration shared task. In *Proceedings of the 3th Named Entity Workshop*, NEWS '11, pages 10–20, Stroudsburg, PA, USA. Association for Computational Linguistics.

Min Zhang, Haizhou Li, A. Kumaran, and Ming Liu. 2012. Report of news 2012 machine transliteration shared task. In *Proceedings of the 4th Named Entity Workshop*, NEWS '12, pages 10–20, Stroudsburg, PA, USA. Association for Computational Linguistics.

Min Zhang, Haizhou Li, A. Kumaranz, and Rafael E. Banchs. 2015. Whitepaper of NEWS 2015 shared task on transliteration generation. In *NEWS '15 Proceedings of the 2015 Named Entities Workshop: Shared Task on Transliteration*, Beijing, China.

Neural Network Transduction Models in Transliteration Generation

Andrew Finch
NICT
3-5 Hikaridai
Keihanna Science City
619-0289 JAPAN
andrew.finch@nict.go.jp

Lemao Liu
NICT
3-5 Hikaridai
Keihanna Science City
619-0289 JAPAN
lmliu@nict.go.jp

Xiaolin Wang
NICT
3-5 Hikaridai
Keihanna Science City
619-0289 JAPAN
xiaolin.wang@nict.go.jp

Eiichiro Sumita
NICT
3-5 Hikaridai
Keihanna Science City
619-0289 JAPAN
eiichiro.sumita@nict.go.jp

Abstract

In this paper we examine the effectiveness of neural network sequence-to-sequence transduction in the task of transliteration generation. In this year's shared evaluation we submitted two systems into all tasks. The primary system was based on the system used for the NEWS 2012 workshop, but was augmented with an additional feature which was the generation probability from a neural network. The secondary system was the neural network model used on its own together with a simple beam search algorithm. Our results show that adding the neural network score as a feature into the phrase-based statistical machine transliteration system was able to increase the performance of the system. In addition, although the neural network alone was not able to match the performance of our primary system (which exploits it), it was able to deliver a respectable performance for most language pairs which is very promising considering the recency of this technique.

1 Introduction

Our primary system for the NEWS shared evaluation on transliteration generation is based on the system entered into the 2012 evaluation (Finch et al., 2012) which in turn was a development of the 2011 system (Finch et al., 2011).

The system is based around the application of phrase-based statistical machine translation (PBSMT) techniques to the task of transliteration, as in (Finch and Sumita, 2008). The system differs from a typical phrase-based machine translation system in a number of important respects:

- Characters rather than words are used as the atomic elements used in the transductive process
- The generative process is constrained to be monotonic. No re-ordering model is used.
- The alignment process is constrained to be monotonic.
  - A non-parametric Bayesian aligner is used instead of GIZA++ and extraction heuristics, to provide a joint alignment/phrase pair induction process.
- The log-linear weights are tuned towards the F-score evaluation metric used in the NEWS evaluation, rather than a machine translation oriented score such as BLEU (Papineni et al., 2001).
- A bilingual language model (Li et al., 2004) is used as a feature during decoding.

An n-best list of hypotheses from the PBSMT system outlined above was then re-scored using the following set of models:

- A maximum entropy model (described in detail in (Finch et al., 2011)).

Proceedings of the Fifth Named Entity Workshop, joint with 53rd ACL and the 7th IJCNLP, pages 61–66,
Beijing, China, July 26-31, 2015. ©2015 Association for Computational Linguistics

- A recurrent neural network RNN target language model (Mikolov et al., 2010).
- An RNN bilingual language model (as in (Finch et al., 2012)).
- A neural network transliteration model (Bahdanau et al., 2014).

The re-scoring was done by extending the log-linear model of the PBSMT system with these 4 additional features. The weights for these features were tuned to maximize F-score in a second tuning step.

The novel aspect of our system in this year's evaluation is the use of a neural network that is capable of performing the entire transductive process. Neural networks capable of sequence-to-sequence transduction where the sequences are of different lengths (Hermann and Blunsom, 2013; Cho et al., 2014a; Bahdanau et al., 2014) are a very recent development in the field of machine translation. We believe this type of approach ought to be well suited to the task of transliteration, which is a task strongly related to that of machine translation but with typically much smaller vocabulary sizes and no problems related to reordering and in most cases no issues relating to out of vocabulary words (characters in our case). On the other hand, it is generally believed (for example (Ellis and Morgan, 1999)) that neural networks can require large amounts of data in order to train effective models, and the data set sizes available in this shared evaluation are quite small, and this lack of data may have caused problems for the neural networks employed.

In all our experiments we have taken a strictly language independent approach. Each of the language pairs were processed automatically from the character sequence representation supplied for the shared tasks, with no language specific treatment for any of the language pairs.

2 System Description

2.1 Non-parametric Bayesian Alignment

To train the joint-source-channel model(s) in our system, we perform a many-to-many sequence alignment. To discover this alignment we use the Bayesian non-parametric technique described in (Finch and Sumita, 2010). Bayesian techniques typically build compact models with few parameters that do not overfit the data and have been shown to be effective for transliteration (Finch and Sumita, 2010; Finch et al., 2011).

2.2 Phrase-based SMT Models

The decoding was performed using a specially modified version of the OCTAVIAN decoder (Finch et al., 2007), an in-house multi-stack phrase-based decoder. The PBSMT component of the system was implemented as a log-linear combination of 4 different models: a joint source-channel model; a target language model; a character insertion penalty mode; and a character sequence pair insertion penalty model. The following sections describe each of these models in detail. Due to the small size of many of the data sets in the shared tasks, we used all of the data to build models for the final systems.

2.2.1 N-gram joint source-channel model

The n-gram joint source-channel model used during decoding by the SMT decoder was trained from the Viterbi alignment arising from the final iteration (30 iterations were used) of the Bayesian segmentation process on the training data. We used the MIT language modeling toolkit (Bo-june et al., 2008) with modified Knesser-Ney smoothing to build this 5-gram model.

2.2.2 N-gram target Language model

The target language model was trained on the target side of the training data. We used the MIT language modeling toolkit with Knesser-Ney smoothing to build this 5-gram model.

2.2.3 Insertion penalty models

Both character based and character-sequence-pair-based insertion penalty models are simple models that add a constant value to their score each time a character (or character sequence pair) is added to the target hypotheses. These models control the tendency both of the joint source-channel model and the target language model to encourage derivations that are too short.

2.3 Re-scoring Step

2.3.1 Overview

The system has a separate re-scoring stage that like the SMT models described in the previous section is implemented as a log-linear model. The log-linear weights are trained using the same MERT (Och, 2003) procedure. In principle, the weights for the models in this stage could be trained in a single step together with the SMT weights (Finch et al., 2011). However the models in this stage are computationally expensive, and to reduce training time we train their weights in a second step. The four models used for re-scoring (20-best) are described in the following sections.

2.3.2 Maximum-entropy model

The maximum entropy model used for re-scoring embodies a set of character and character-sequence based features designed to take the local context of source and target characters and character sequences into account; the reader is referred to (Finch et al., 2011) for a full description of this model.

2.3.3 RNN Language models

We introduce two RNN language models (Mikolov et al., 2011) into the re-scoring step of our system. The first model is a language model over character sequences in the target language; the second model is a joint source-channel model over bilingual character sequence pairs. These models were trained on the same data as their n-gram counterparts described in Sections 2.2.1 and 2.2.2. The models were trained using the training procedure described in (Finch et al., 2012).

2.3.4 Neural network transliteration model

The neural network transliteration model was trained directly from the source and target sequences themselves. The model used in tuning was trained only on the training data set; the model used for the final submission was trained on all of the data. The neural network software was developed using the GroundHog neural machine translation toolkit (Cho et al., 2014b), built on top of Theano (Bergstra et al., 2010; Bastien et al., 2012). For all of the experiments we used the same neural network architecture which was the default architecture supplied with the toolkit. That is, we used networks of 1000 hidden units and used the RNNSearch technique reported in (Bahdanau et al., 2014). In a set of pilot experiments we evaluated a number of neural network models with fewer parameters on development data, under the hypothesis that these would be more suitable for the task of transliteration. However, the best results came from the default set of parameters, and therefore these were used in all runs. Due to the resources required to train the neural network models only a few experiments were able to be performed and only on the English-Katakana task. It may be the case that different architectures could lead to in significantly higher performance than the results we obtained, and this remains an area for future research. The neural networks were trained for 50,000 iterations based on the analysis of the convergence of the performance on development data of a network trained on the English-Katakana task. The models took from 1 to 9 days to train, depending on the language pair, on a single core of a Tesla K40 GPU.

2.4 Parameter Tuning

The exponential log-linear model weights of both the SMT and re-scoring stages of our system were set by tuning the system on development data using the MERT procedure (Och, 2003) by means of the publicly available ZMERT toolkit [1] (Zaidan, 2009). The systems reported in this paper used a metric based on the word-level F-score, an official evaluation metric for the shared tasks (Zhang et al., 2012), which measures the relationship of the longest common subsequence of the transliteration pair to the lengths of both source and target sequences.

3 Evaluation Results

The official scores for our system are given in Table 1. It is interesting to compare the results of the 2012 system with the results from this year's primary submission on the 2012 test set, since these results show the effect of adding the neural network transliteration scores into the re-scorer. In 11 out of 14 of the runs, the system's performance was improved, and for some language pairs, notably En-He, En-Hi, En-Ka, En-Pe, En-Ta, En-Th, Th-En and Jn-Jk the improvement was substantial. The using the neural network model scores was ineffective for Ar-En, Ch-En and En-Ch. Ar-En was surprising as the training corpus size for this task was considerably larger than for any other task, and we expected this to benefit the neural network approach. Overall however, it is clear from the results that the neural network re-scoring was very effective and the effect was considerably greater than that from the RNN re-scoring models introduced in the 2012 system.

The results on the Jn-Jk task were surprising. The neural network transliteration system alone produced very low accuracy scores, but when used in combination with the PBSMT system gave a 9.7% increase in top-1 accuracy. One particular characteristic of this data set is the disparity in length between the sequences; kanji sequences were very short whereas the romanized form was much longer. Visual inspection of the output from

[1] http://www.cs.jhu.edu/~ozaidan/zmert/

Language Pair		2012 system	Primary 2012	Primary 2011	Secondary 2012	Secondary 2011
Arabic to English	(ArEn)	0.588	0.529	0.527	0.469	0.494
English to Bengali	(EnBa)	0.460	0.483	0.479	0.364	0.375
Chinese to English	(ChEn)	0.203	0.184	0.158	0.136	0.115
English to Chinese	(EnCh)	0.311	0.313	0.344	0.220	0.213
English to Hebrew	(EnHe)	0.154	0.179	0.609	0.163	0.558
English to Hindi	(EnHi)	0.668	0.696	0.474	0.641	0.410
English to Japanese Katakana	(EnJa)	0.401	0.407	0.412	0.338	0.399
English to Kannada	(EnKa)	0.546	0.562	0.412	0.546	0.360
English to Korean Hangul	(EnKo)	0.384	0.363	0.365	0.189	0.200
English to Persian	(EnPe)	0.655	0.697	0.360	0.565	0.329
English to Tamil	(EnTa)	0.592	0.626	0.474	0.584	0.406
English to Thai	(EnTh)	0.122	0.157	0.387	0.132	0.359
English to Japanese Kanji	(JnJk)	0.513	0.610	0.452	0.032	0.035
Thai to English	(ThEn)	0.140	0.154	0.277	0.129	0.178

Table 1: The evaluation results on the 2015 shared task for our systems in terms of the top-1 accuracy.

the direct neural network transliteration showed that the output sequences derived from the roman character sequences, but were too long. When integrated with the PBSMT system, output sequences of this form were not a problem as they were rarely generated as candidates for re-scoring.

We conducted two experiments in the reverse direction from Jk to Jn. The first was based on a neural network transliteration system from character to character in the same manner as the secondary submission. The second system was a neural network that transduced from character to character sequence. We used a 1-to-many sequence alignment induced by the Bayesian aligner to train this model. The character-to-character system had a top-1 accuracy of 0.245, the character-to-character sequence system had a top-1 accuracy of 0.305. These results indicate that the neural network is capable of generating long sequences from short sequences with reasonably high accuracy, and that there may be something to be gained by using phrasal units in the neural network transduction process, as was the case when moving from word-based models to phrase-based models in machine translation.

4 Conclusion

The system used for this year's shared evaluation was implemented within a phrase-based statistical machine translation framework augmented by a bilingual language model trained from a many-to-many alignment from a non-parametric Bayesian aligner. The system had a re-scoring step that integrated features from a maximum entropy model, a target RNN language model, a bilingual RNN language model, and a neural network transliteration model.

Our results showed that the neural network transliteration model was a very effective component in the re-scoring stage of our system that substantially improved the performance of our system over the 2012 system for most language pairs. Furthermore, the neural network transliterator was a capable system in its own right on most of the tasks, and equaled or exceeded the performance of our 2012 system on 3 language pairs. These results are particularly impressive considering that this line of research is relatively new, and we believe neural network transliteration models will have a bright future in this field.

Acknowledgements

For the English-Japanese, English-Korean and Arabic-English datasets, the reader is referred to the CJK website: http://www.cjk.org. For English-Hindi, English-Tamil, and English-Kannada, and English-Bangla the data sets originated from the work of (Kumaran and Kellner, 2007) [2]. The Chinese language corpora came from the Xinhua news agency (Xinhua News Agency, 1992). The English Persian corpus originates from the work of (Karimi et al., 2006; Karimi et al., 2007).

[2]http://research.microsoft.com/india

References

Dzmitry Bahdanau, Kyunghyun Cho, and Yoshua Bengio. 2014. Neural machine translation by jointly learning to align and translate. *CoRR*.

Frédéric Bastien, Pascal Lamblin, Razvan Pascanu, James Bergstra, Ian J. Goodfellow, Arnaud Bergeron, Nicolas Bouchard, and Yoshua Bengio. 2012. Theano: new features and speed improvements. Deep Learning and Unsupervised Feature Learning NIPS 2012 Workshop.

James Bergstra, Olivier Breuleux, Frédéric Bastien, Pascal Lamblin, Razvan Pascanu, Guillaume Desjardins, Joseph Turian, David Warde-Farley, and Yoshua Bengio. 2010. Theano: a CPU and GPU math expression compiler. In *Proceedings of the Python for Scientific Computing Conference (SciPy)*, June. Oral Presentation.

Bo-june, Paul Hsu, and James Glass. 2008. Iterative language model estimation: Efficient data structure and algorithms. In *Proc. Interspeech*.

Kyunghyun Cho, Bart van Merriënboer, Dzmitry Bahdanau, and Yoshua Bengio. 2014a. On the properties of neural machine translation: Encoder-decoder approaches. *CoRR*.

Kyunghyun Cho, Bart van Merrienboer, Çaglar Gülçehre, Fethi Bougares, Holger Schwenk, and Yoshua Bengio. 2014b. Learning phrase representations using RNN encoder-decoder for statistical machine translation. *CoRR*.

Dan Ellis and Nelson Morgan. 1999. Size matters: An empirical study of neural network training for large vocabulary continuous speech recognition. In *Acoustics, Speech, and Signal Processing, 1999. Proceedings., 1999 IEEE International Conference on*, volume 2, pages 1013–1016. IEEE.

Andrew Finch and Eiichiro Sumita. 2008. Phrase-based machine transliteration. In *Proceedings of the 3rd International Joint Conference on Natural Language Processing (IJCNLP)*, volume 1, Hyderabad, India.

Andrew Finch and Eiichiro Sumita. 2010. A Bayesian Model of Bilingual Segmentation for Transliteration. In Marcello Federico, Ian Lane, Michael Paul, and François Yvon, editors, *Proceedings of the seventh International Workshop on Spoken Language Translation (IWSLT)*, pages 259–266.

Andrew Finch, Etienne Denoual, Hideo Okuma, Michael Paul, Hirofumi Yamamoto, Keiji Yasuda, Ruiqiang Zhang, and Eiichiro Sumita. 2007. The NICT/ATR speech translation system for IWSLT 2007. In *Proceedings of the IWSLT*, Trento, Italy.

Andrew Finch, Paul Dixon, and Eiichiro Sumita. 2011. Integrating models derived from non-parametric bayesian co-segmentation into a statistical machine transliteration system. In *Proceedings of the Named Entities Workshop*, pages 23–27, Chiang Mai, Thailand, Nov. Asian Federation of Natural Language Processing.

Andrew Finch, Paul Dixon, and Eiichiro Sumita. 2012. Rescoring a phrase-based machine transliteration system with recurrent neural network language models. In *Proceedings of the 4th Named Entity Workshop (NEWS) 2012*, pages 47–51, Jeju, Korea, July. Association for Computational Linguistics.

Karl Moritz Hermann and Phil Blunsom. 2013. A simple model for learning multilingual compositional semantics. *CoRR*, abs/1312.6173.

Sarvnaz Karimi, Andrew Turpin, and Falk Scholer. 2006. English to persian transliteration. In *SPIRE*, pages 255–266.

Sarvnaz Karimi, Andrew Turpin, and Falk Scholer. 2007. Corpus effects on the evaluation of automated transliteration systems. *Proceedings of the 45th Annual Meeting of the Association of Computational Linguistics*.

A. Kumaran and Tobias Kellner. 2007. A generic framework for machine transliteration. In *SIGIR '07*, pages 721–722.

Haizhou Li, Min Zhang, and Jian Su. 2004. A joint source-channel model for machine transliteration. In *ACL '04: Proceedings of the 42nd Annual Meeting on Association for Computational Linguistics*, page 159, Morristown, NJ, USA. Association for Computational Linguistics.

Tomáš Mikolov, Martin Karafiát, Lukáš Burget, Jan Černocký, and Sanjeev Khudanpur. 2010. Recurrent neural network based language model. In *Proceedings of the 11th Annual Conference of the International Speech Communication Association (INTERSPEECH 2010)*, number 9, pages 1045–1048. International Speech Communication Association.

Tomáš Mikolov, Anoop Deoras, Stefan Kombrink, Lukáš Burget, and Jan Černocký. 2011. Empirical evaluation and combination of advanced language modeling techniques. In *Proceedings of Interspeech 2011*, number 8, pages 605–608. International Speech Communication Association.

Franz J. Och. 2003. Minimum error rate training for statistical machine translation. In *Proceedings of the 41st Meeting of the Association for Computational Linguistics (ACL 2003)*, Sapporo, Japan.

K. Papineni, S. Roukos, T. Ward, and W.J. Zhu. 2001. *Bleu: a Method for Automatic Evaluation of Machine Translation.* IBM Research Report rc22176 (w0109022), Thomas J. Watson Research Center.

Xinhua News Agency. 1992. Chinese transliteration of foreign personal names. *The Commercial Press*.

Omar F. Zaidan. 2009. Z-MERT: A fully configurable open source tool for minimum error rate training of machine translation systems. *The Prague Bulletin of Mathematical Linguistics*, 91:79–88.

Min Zhang, Haizhou Li, Liu Ming, and A. Kumaran. 2012. Whitepaper of news 2012 shared task on machine transliteration. In *Proceedings of the 2012 Named Entities Workshop*, Jeju, Korea. Association for Computational Linguistics.

A Hybrid Transliteration Model for Chinese/English Named Entities —BJTU-NLP Report for the 5th Named Entities Workshop

Dandan Wang, Xiaohui Yang, Jinan Xu, Yufeng Chen, Nan Wang, Bojia Liu, Jian Yang, Yujie Zhang
School of Computer and Information Technology
Beijing Jiaotong University
{13120427, xhyang, jaxu, chenyf, 14120428, 14125181, 13120441, yjzhang}@bjtu.edu.cn

Abstract

This paper presents our system (BJTU-NLP system) for the NEWS2015 evaluation task of Chinese-to-English and English-to-Chinese named entity transliteration. Our system adopts a hybrid machine transliteration approach, which combines several features. To further improve the result, we adopt external data extracted from wikipeda to expand the training set. In addition, pre-processing and post-processing rules are utilized to further improve the performance. The final performance on the test corpus shows that our system achieves comparable results with other state-of-the-art systems.

1 Introduction

Machine transliteration transforms the script of a word from a source language to a target language automatically. Knight(1998) proposes a phoneme-based approach to solve the transliteration between English names and Japanese katakana. The phoneme-based approach needs a pronunciation dictionary for one or two languages. These dictionaries usually do not exist or can't cover all the names. Jia(2009) views machine transliteration as a special example of machine translation and uses the phrase-based machine translation model to solve it. However, using the English letters and Chinese characters as basic mapping units will make ambiguity in the alignment and translation step. Huang(2011) proposes a novel nonparametric Bayesian using synchronous adaptor grammars to model the grapheme-based transliteration.

This paper describes a machine transliteration system and data measures for participating NEWS2015 evaluation, which is abbreviated as BJTU-NLP. We participated in two transliteration masks: Chinese-to-English and English-to-Chinese named entity transliteration task. This report briefly introduces the implementation framework of our machine transliteration system, and analyzes the experimental results over the evaluation data.

The following parts are organized as follows: Section 2 briefly introduces the implementation framework of the transliteration system. Section 3 introduces the details of the experiment and data processing in brief. In Section 4, experimental results are given and the results of the experiment are analyzed. Section 5 is our conclusion and future work.

2 System Description

By treating transliteration as a translation problem, BJTU-NLP has realized a machine transliteration system based on the combination of multiple features by a log-linear model, to complete the corresponding experiments with English-Chinese and Chinese-English name pairs

The description of the whole transliteration system is as follows.

2.1 A Log-linear Machine Transliteration Model

In this evaluation, a tool is used in our machine transliteration system based on the fusion multiple features. In this system, we introduce a linear log model for transliteration (Koehn et al., 2007), using combination features in it. The process of transliteration can be described as follows: for a given source language name $\boldsymbol{s}$ find the optimal result $\hat{\boldsymbol{e}}$ from all possible results $\boldsymbol{e}$, which is computed by:

$$\hat{\boldsymbol{e}} = \arg\max_e \frac{\exp\left(\sum_{m=1}^{M} \lambda_m h_m(e,s)\right)}{\sum_{e'} \exp\left(\sum_{m=1}^{M} \lambda_m h_m(e',s)\right)} \quad (1)$$

Proceedings of the Fifth Named Entity Workshop, joint with 53rd ACL and the 7th IJCNLP, pages 67–71,
Beijing, China, July 26-31, 2015. ©2015 Association for Computational Linguistics

Where M is the number of used features, $h_m(\boldsymbol{e},\boldsymbol{s})$ is the *mth* transliteration feature, and λ_m is the weight of the *mth* transliteration feature.

2.2 Features

In the transliteration process, the source name is transformed from left to right in the order, lexical reordering problem does not exist, therefore, the transliteration model does not require replacement model features, and because "phrase translation pair" does not exist lexical correspondence (between English letters and correspondence Chinese characters), forward/reverse phrase lexicalization probability are not used in our transliteration model. In the final, the features we used are as follow:

1. Forward phrase translation probability, $P(e|s)$ is the probability of translating into English name ***e*** from Chinese name ***s***, the formula is as follows.
$$P(e|s) = \frac{count(e,s)}{count_{\bar{e}}(e,s)} \quad (2)$$
2. Reverse phrase translation probability, $P(s|e)$ is the probability of translating into Chinese name ***s*** from English name ***e*** , the formula is as follows.
$$P(s|e) = \frac{count(s,e)}{count_{\bar{f}}(e,s)} \quad (3)$$
3. The length of name
4. The normalized length deviation after transforming the length of the other language into the reference language, $I(e|s)$, $I(s|e)$ are computed as follows.
$$I(e|s) = \frac{|len(s)-len(e)|}{len(s)} \quad (4)$$
$$I(s|e) = \frac{|len(e)-len(s)|}{len(e)} \quad (5)$$
Where *len(s)* is the number of characters this source name contains, *len(e)* is the number of segments target name contains.
5. Language model score, $lm(c)$. In the translation model based on phrase, each source phrase fragments can be translated without considering the source language phrase fragments which are in front of it. Each source language phrases are independent in transliteration, the transliteration between source language phrase and target language phrase only rely on the language model of the target language.

2.3 Parameter Tuning and Decoding

The system adopts GIZA++, which is a word alignment model to extract transliteration phrases pairs. In order to get the best weight of features and the best name transliteration model, the process of parameter tuning is as follows:

1. The weights of five features mentioned in the previous section are initialized to 1.
2. Using the log-linear model on the development set, we can obtain the NBest transliteration candidate, then merge with the original NBest candidate to form new candidate results.
3. According to the new NBest candidate results obtained, in order to get the best BLEU value, each feature weight is adjusted with the ZMERT (Zaidan et al.2009) toolkit for a better log-linear model.
4. Repeat steps 2, 3 until the model reaches convergence, finally we obtain the optimal weight of each feature. Then decode given names, using phrase table formed in training stage and transliteration model with optimal weight.

3 Rule-based Adaptation

3.1 External Dictionary

In this evaluation, in addition to the official data sets, we proposed to import the Wikipedia data set as an external dictionary. After obtaining the data from the Wikipedia database, we use clustering and iterative methods to obtain named entity pairs. We did data cleansing, de-noising and de-emphasis for the obtained name entity pairs. For the reserved data, it need to comply with the following requirements:

1. Retain only the English and Chinese name transliterations.
2. For some English names contains a modified letter, for example Áá, Àà, Ăă, Ắắ, we would replace the letter with its corresponding ordinary alphabet letters.
3. Cannot have duplicate transliteration results (including given official data sets).

After the above steps, we got about 37,151 available named entity pairs. During the expanded training of non-standardized methods, we need to add the above corpus into English-to-Chinese and Chinese-to-English training set respectively, and then do the de-emphasis operation to ensure the uniqueness of each named entity pair.

3.2 Chinese-to-English preprocessing

For Chinese corpus, our preprocessing rules are as follows:

1. Simplified Chinese representation

2. Chinese word segmentation method

Segmentation

During the segmentation stage, we take the given word as a sequence of characters. Then combined with the characteristics of Chinese grammar, we take particular rule to Chinese word segmentation as divide the Chinese word by space.

Word Alignment

Word alignment here accurately refers to the alignment of segmentation result of the above step result. Word alignment tool we used is the GIZA ++ (Och et al., 2003). Since the corpus is named entity pairs, we took the result of GIZA ++ as the final word alignments.

Language Model

After several times comparison test, the two systems involved in this evaluation adopt the 3-gram language model.

3.3 English-to-Chinese preprocessing

For English corpus, our preprocessing rules are as follows:

1. Capitalization representation
2. English word segmentation method

Segmentation

During this segmentation stage, we also take the given word as a sequence of characters. Then we take particular rules to English word segmentation as divide these words by syllable.

Word Alignment

Word alignment here uses the same tool as above.

Language Model

The two systems involved in this evaluation also adopt the 3-gram language model.

3.4 Corpus usage

The evaluation directions of our participation are Chinese-to-English and English-to-Chinese named entity transliteration direction. And all evaluation corpus we used for this evaluation (including the training sets, development sets, test sets and reference sets) are as follows:

	Training Set	Dev Set	Test Set
English-to-Chinese	37,753	2,802	1008
Chinese-to-English	28,678	2,719	1019

Table 1 standardized methods of data list

	Training Set	Dev Set	Test Set
English-to-Chinese	74,904	2,802	1008
Chinese-to-English	65,829	2,719	1019

Table 2 Non-standardized methods of data list

4 Experiments

4.1 Data Sets

The standard training set of English-Chinese transliteration track contains 37753 pairs of names. We pick up 37151 pairs of names extracted from Wikipedia to merge into the training set. 2802 pairs are treated as the final dev set to tune the weights of system features. For the Chinese-English back transliteration track, the final training and test sets are formed in the same way. The official dev set is used directly.

The Srilm (Stolcke et al., 2002) toolkit is used to count n-gram on the target of the training set. Here we use a 3-gram language model. In the transliteration model training step, the Giza++ (Och et al., 2003) generates the alignment with the grow-diag-and-final heuristic, while other setup is default. The following 4 metrics are used to measure the quality of the transliteration results (Li et al., 2009a): Word Accuracy in Top-1 (ACC), Fuzziness in Top-1 (Mean F-score), Mean Reciprocal Rank (MRR), MAPref.

4.2 Experimental results

Our transliteration systems' outputs have following format problems:

1. English-to-Chinese outputs: the Chinese output words are still separated by spaces
2. Chinese-to-English outputs: English output words are still divided by syllable

To solve these problems, we make the following amendments to the outputs:

1. Remove the spaces between character and character, syllable and syllable
2. The English results are expressed as: initial capital letters, other letter lowercase

We adopt Niutrans (Xiao et al., 2012) to realize our log-linear model to combining several features. By comparing the experiment, we found that segmentation by syllable of English words is more effective and segmentation by Pinyin and syllable of Chinese words performs better. We adopt the above standard and non-standard training set to evaluate the official test set, and use official development set to adjust parameters. The evaluation results of the standard and non-standard training set and corresponding analysis are shown as follows.

4.2.1 Evaluation Results and Analysis of Standard Training Set

We evaluated the four official test sets respectively. We calculated the four parameter values, ACC, F-score, MRR and MAP_ref, according to the four official evaluation standards. The experimental results are shown in Table 3.

Test Sets	ACC	F-score	MRR	MAP_ref
ChEn_2266	0.151	0.766	0.151	0.151
ChEn_1019	0.157	0.732	0.157	0.151
EnCh_2000	0.225	0.620	0.225	0.212
EnCh_1008	0.204	0.605	0.204	0.195

Table 3 Standard training set evaluation results

In Table 3, we found that the effect of English-Chinese transliteration is better than the Chinese-English transliteration. The effect of English-Chinese transliteration is better than the Chinese-English transliteration, which shows that segmentation of syllable is more reasonable for preprocessing when the source language is English, and preprocessing method of Chinese needs to be improved.

4.2.2 Evaluation Results and Analysis of non-Standard Training Set

We added the English-Chinese and Chinese-English named entities drawn from the Wikipedia to the training set, and evaluate the official test sets by the expanded training set as non-Standard training set. We calculated the four official parameter values likewise and experimental results are shown in Table 4.

Test Sets	ACC	F-score	MRR	MAP_ref
ChEn_2266	0.105	0.746	0.105	0.105
ChEn_1019	0.157	0.732	0.157	0.151
EnCh_2000	0.224	0.629	0.224	0.212
EnCh_1008	0.193	0.605	0.193	0.182

Table 4 non-Standard training set evaluation results

We can conclude from Table 4 that the results of the evaluation on the non-Standard training set have promotion over that on the Standard training set. This suggests that increasing the training set has a positive influence on improving the evaluating results.

5 Conclusions and Future Work

This paper mainly describes the machine transliteration system and data measures for participating NEWS2015 evaluation of BJTU-NLP. We adopt a hybrid transliteration model to realize named entities transliteration. In the process of training, we added the preprocessing of training corpus, modified related parameters of Niutrans system and the compared results of the experiment with different parameters. Related post-processing is also added according to the transliteration results. Simultaneously, we expand the training set with the help of Wikipedia in the named entities. The experimental results show that after joining in the named entities to Wikipedia, the evaluating results have a certain increase.

As to future work, we plan to conduct in-depth research and discussion in the preprocessing of named entities transliteration, post-processing and machine transliteration model, etc.

Acknowledgement

The research work has been supported by the National Nature Science Foundation of China under grant no. 61370130, and 61473294, the Fundamental Research Funds for the Central Universities (2014RC040), and also the International Science & Technology Cooperation Program of China under grant No. 2014DFA11350.

Reference

Keven Knight, Jonathan Graehl. 1998. Machine Transliteration. Computational Linguistics, Vol. 24, No. 4, pp. 599-612.

Tong Xiao, Jingbo Zhu, Hao Zhang and Qiang Li. 2012. NiuTrans: An Open Source Toolkit for Phrase-based and Syntax-based Machine Translation. In Proc. of ACL, demonstration session.

Andreas Stolcke. 2002. SRILM - an Extensible Language Modeling Toolkit. In Proc. Of ICSLP, Denver, USA.

Franz Josef Och, Hermann Ney. 2003. A systematic comparison of various statistical alignment models. Comput.Linguistics 29, 1, 19-51.

Yun Huang, Min Zhang and Chewlim Tan. 2011. Nonparametric Bayesian Machine Transliteration with Synchronous Adaptor Grammars. In Proceedings of ACL-HLT 2011: Short Papers, Portland, Oregon, pp.534-539.

Yuxiang Jia, Danqing Zhu, and Shiwen Y. 2009. A Noisy Channel Model for Grapheme-based Machine Transliteration. In the Proceedings of the 2009 Named Entities Workshop, 2009, pp. 88-91.

Koehn P, Och F J, Marcu D. Statistical Phrase-Based Translation[J]. Statistical Phrase-Based Translation, 2002, (5):127--133.

Zaidan O. Z-MERT: A fully configurable open source tool for minimum error rate training of machine translation systems[C]. //Prague Bulletin of Mathematical Linguistics. 2010:2009.

Multiple System Combination for Transliteration

Garrett Nicolai, Bradley Hauer, Mohammad Salameh,
Adam St Arnaud, Ying Xu, Lei Yao, Grzegorz Kondrak
Department of Computing Science
University of Alberta, Edmonton, Canada
{nicolai,bmhauer,msalameh,ajstarna,
yx2,lyao1,gkondrak}@ualberta.ca

Abstract

We report the results of our experiments in the context of the NEWS 2015 Shared Task on Transliteration. We focus on methods of combining multiple base systems, and leveraging transliterations from multiple languages. We show error reductions over the best base system of up to 10% when using supplemental transliterations, and up to 20% when using system combination. We also discuss the quality of the shared task datasets.

1 Introduction

The 2015 NEWS Shared Task on Machine Transliteration continues the series of shared tasks that were held yearly between 2009 and 2012. With the exception of the 2010 edition that included transliteration mining, the task has been limited to learning transliteration models from the training sets of word pairs. Participants are allowed to use target lexicons or monolingual corpora, but since those are "non-standard", the results are not comparable across different teams. Another drawback of the current framework is the lack of context that is required to account for morphological alterations.

Our University of Alberta team has participated in each of the five editions of this shared task. Although this year's task is virtually identical to the 2012 task, there has been progress in transliteration research since then. In particular, transliteration projects at the University of Alberta have led to the design of novel techniques for leveraging supplemental information such as phonetic transcriptions and transliterations from other languages. During those projects, we also observed that combinations of diverse systems often outperform their component systems. We decided to test this hypothesis in the current rerun of the NEWS shared task.

In this paper, we describe experiments that involve three well-known transliteration approaches. DIRECTL+, SEQUITUR, and statistical machine translation toolkits (SMT). In an effort to harness the strengths of each system, we explore various techniques of combining their outputs. Furthermore, we experiment with leveraging transliterations from other languages, in order to test whether this can improve the overall results. We obtain state-of-the-art results on most language pairs.

2 Base Systems

In this section, we describe our three base systems: DIRECTL+, SEQUITUR, and SMT.

2.1 DirecTL+

DIRECTL+ is a publicly-available[1] discriminative string transduction tool, which was initially developed for grapheme-to-phoneme conversion (Jiampojamarn et al., 2008). DIRECTL+ was successfully applied to transliteration in the previous NEWS shared tasks by our team (Jiampojamarn et al., 2009; Jiampojamarn et al., 2010b; Bhargava et al., 2011; Kondrak et al., 2012), as well as by other teams (Okuno, 2012; Wu et al., 2012). We make use of all features described by Jiampojamarn et al. (2010a). We perform source-target pair alignment with *mpaligner* (Kubo et al., 2011) because it performed slightly better in our development experiments than M2M-aligner (Jiampojamarn et al., 2007). The parameters of the transducer and the aligner were tuned separately for each language pair.

2.2 SEQUITUR

SEQUITUR is a joint n-gram-based string transduction system[2] originally designed for grapheme-to-phoneme transduction (Bisani and Ney, 2008), which is also applicable to a wide

[1] *https://code.google.com/p/directl-p*
[2] *http://www-i6.informatik.rwth-aachen.de/web/Software*

Proceedings of the Fifth Named Entity Workshop, joint with 53rd ACL and the 7th IJCNLP, pages 72–77,
Beijing, China, July 26-31, 2015. ©2015 Association for Computational Linguistics

variety of monotone translation tasks including transliteration (Finch and Sumita, 2010; Nejad et al., 2011). Unlike DIRECTL+, which requires aligned source-target pairs, SEQUITUR directly trains a joint n-gram model for transduction from unaligned data. Higher order n-gram models are trained iteratively: a unigram model is created first; this model is then used to train a bigram model, which is then in turn used to train a trigram model, and so on. The order of the model trained is a parameter tuned on a development set.

An important limitation of SEQUITUR is that both the source and target character sets are limited to a maximum of 255 symbols each. This precludes a direct application of SEQUITUR to scripts such as Chinese, Korean, and Japanese Kanji. Ultimately, it was a factor in our decision to leave out the datasets that involve these languages.

2.3 SMT

We frame the transliteration task as a machine translation task by treating individual characters as words, and sequences of characters as phrases. We align the word pairs with GIZA++ (Och and Ney, 2003), and use Moses (Koehn et al., 2007), a phrase-based SMT system, to generate transliterations. The decoder's log-linear model includes a standard feature set. Four translation model features encode phrase translation probabilities and lexical scores in both directions. Both alignment and generation are monotonic, i.e. reordering is disabled, with distortion limit set to zero. We train a KN-smoothed 5-gram language model on the target side of the parallel training data with SRILM (Stolcke, 2002). If a source word is provided with several target transliterations, we select the first one. The decoder's log-linear model is tuned with MERT (Och, 2003). We use BLEU score (Papineni et al., 2002) as an evaluation metric during tuning.

3 Language-specific Preprocessing

Our development experiments showed that romanization of Chinese and Japanese characters can be helpful.

For the alignment of English and Chinese (EnCh) names, we convert the Chinese names in the training data into Pinyin romanization, as described in Kondrak et al. (2012). This set of training pairs is aligned using our many-to-many aligner, and the resulting alignment links are projected onto Chinese characters. In cases where alignments split individual Chinese characters, they are expanded to include the entire character. Finally, the generation model is derived from the alignment between English letters to Chinese characters.

For English-to-Japanese (EnJa) transliteration, the Katakana symbols are first converted to Latin characters following a deterministic mapping, as described in Jiampojamarn et al. (2009). The English characters are aligned to the Latin characters, and a generation model is learned from the alignments. At test time, the model outputs Latin symbols, which are converted back into Japanese Katakana. We employed a similar approach for SEQUITUR.

4 System Combination

Each of our base systems can generate n-best lists of predictions, together with confidence scores. We experimented with several methods of combining the outputs of the base systems.

4.1 LINCOMB

We generate the n-best transliterations for each test input, and combine the lists via a linear combination of the confidence scores. Scores are first normalized according to the following formula:

$$normScore = \frac{(score - minScore)}{(maxScore - minScore)}$$

where $minScore$ is the confidence score of the n-th best prediction, and $maxScore$ is the confidence score of the best prediction. Predictions that do not occur in a specific system's n-best predictions are also given a score of 0 for combination. n is set to 10 in all of our experiments. If an n-best list contains less than 10 predictions, $minScore$ is set to the score of the last prediction in the list. Our development experiments indicated that this method of combination was more accurate than a simpler method that uses only the prediction ranks.

4.2 RERANK

Bhargava and Kondrak (2012) propose a reranking approach to transliteration to leverage supplemental representations, such as phonetic transcriptions and transliterations from other languages. The reranker utilizes many features, including the similarity of the candidate outputs to the supplemental representations, several types of n-gram features, and the confidence scores of the base system itself. Once a feature vector is created for each output, weights are learned with an SVM reranker.

Bhargava et al. (2011) apply the reranking approach (RERANK) to system combination. The idea is to rerank the n-best list output from a base system, using the top prediction from another system. If the correct output is in the n-best list, reranking has the potential to elevate it to the top. The paper reports a 5% relative increase in accuracy on EnHi with DIRECTL+ and SEQUITUR as the base and supplemental system, respectively.

For this shared task, we investigated two modifications of RERANK. First, we attempted to extend the original approach to take advantage of more than one supplemental system. For this purpose, we experimented with *cascaded reranking*, in which the n-best list is reranked using the top outputs of both supplemental systems in turn. Second, in an attempt to emulate the effectiveness of the linear combination approach, we experimented with restricting the set of features to confidence scores from the individual systems.

4.3 JOINT

Yao and Kondrak (2015) propose a JOINT generation approach that can incorporate multiple transliterations as input, and show that it outperforms the reranking approach of Bhargava and Kondrak (2012). The JOINT system is a modified version of DIRECTL+ that utilizes aligned supplemental transliterations to learn additional features. Supplemental transliterations are then provided to the system at test time, in order to generate the final output.

For this shared task, we performed two sets of experiments with the JOINT system. While the JOINT system was designed to incorporate additional transliterations as supplemental information, we were also interested if it could be used for system combination. For this purpose, we provided the JOINT system with the output of all three base systems as supplemental inputs. In addition, we experimented with attaching distinct tags to each character in the supplemental inputs, in order to make a distinction between the symbols produced by different supplemental systems. The JOINT system was trained on a held-out set composed of the outputs of the base systems generated for each source word.

	DTL	SEQ	SMT	LINCOMB
ArEn	51.4	45.9	47.1	**57.1**
EnBa	37.1	37.8	34.9	**40.1**
EnCh	29.4	–	27.9	**29.7**
EnHe	**61.3**	56.6	53.1	60.1
EnHi	43.5	40.4	36.8	**45.4**
EnJa	38.9	35.8	31.8	**40.3**
EnKa	32.7	35.7	28.1	**37.4**
EnPe	**34.7**	32.0	29.0	34.6
EnTa	**38.5**	34.4	29.3	38.4
EnTh	36.2	35.8	30.6	**39.5**
ThEn	33.2	36.5	34.3	**39.5**

Table 1: Transliteration accuracy of DIRECTL+, SEQUITUR, and SMT on the development sets.

The second set of experiments followed the original design of Yao and Kondrak (2015), in which the supplemental data consists of transliterations of a source word in other languages. We extracted the supplemental transliterations from the NEWS 2015 Shared Task training and development sets for which English was the source language. For words with no supplemental transliterations, we fall back on base DIRECTL+ output.

5 Development Experiments

For our development experiments, we randomly split the provided training sets into ten equal folds, of which eight were used for base system training, and one for base system tuning, with the final fold held out for system combination training. The base models were trained without language-specific preprocessing.

Table 1 shows the results on the provided development set. DIRECTL+ is the best performing base system on eight datasets, with SEQUITUR winning on the remaining three. Although SMT is never the best, it comes second on three tasks. The absolute differences between the three system are within 10%.

Because of its simplicity, we expected LINCOMB to serve as the baseline combination method. However, as shown in Table 1, it performs surprisingly well, providing an improvement over the best base system on eight out of eleven datasets. An additional advantage of LINCOMB is that it requires no training or parameter tuning. Since the other two combination methods are more complicated and less reliable, we chose LINCOMB as our default method.

	NEWS 2011	NEWS 2012
ArEn	**61.7**	**59.6**
EnBa	**50.9**	**49.2**
EnCh	33.2	31.4
EnHe	**62.2**	**18.0**
EnHi	**48.8**	64.9
EnJa	**42.5**	39.7
EnKa	**43.4**	54.5
EnPe	36.1	**71.0**
EnTa	**47.7**	58.5
EnTh	**41.0**	14.1
ThEn	27.3	**15.6**

Table 2: Official test results for standard linear combination (LINCOMB).

Some configurations of RERANK did achieve improvements over the best base system on most sets, but the results were generally below LINCOMB. This confirms the observation of (Bhargava and Kondrak, 2012) that LINCOMB is a strong combination baseline because it utilizes entire n-best lists from all systems.

The JOINT approach was unable to improve over base DIRECTL+ when trained on relatively small held-out sets. We also tried to leverage the entire training set for this purpose using 10-cross validation. However, that method requires a substantial amount of time and computing resources, and after disappointing initial results on selected datasets, we decided to forgo further experimentation. It remains an open question whether the joint generation approach can be made to work as a system combination.

The JOINT approach performs much better in its original setup, in which additional transliterations from other languages are provided as input. However, its effectiveness depends on the amount of supplemental information that is available per source word. The improvement of JOINT over base DIRECTL+ seems to be correlated with the percentage of words with at least two supplemental transliterations in the corresponding test set. The language pairs with over 50% of such words in the development set include EnHi, EnKa, and EnTa.

6 Test Results

Table 2 shows the official test results for LINCOMB. Following our development results, we designated LINCOMB for our primary runs except on EnHe, EnPe, and EnTa, where DIRECTL+ was chosen instead (see the results in Table 3). Overall, our standard runs achieved top results on 14 out of 22 datasets.

Table 3 includes our remaining test results. We submitted the JOINT runs on languages that had promising improvements in the development results. These runs were designated as non-standard even though the supplemental transliterations are from the provided NEWS datasets. For these languages, we also submitted standard DIRECTL+ runs, in order to gauge the improvement obtained by JOINT. The JOINT outperformed base DIRECTL+ on six out of eight datasets.

	NEWS 2011		NEWS 2012	
	DTL	JOINT	DTL	JOINT
EnHe	**62.2**	61.6	17.4	**18.4**
EnHi	47.7	**53.1**	55.8	55.9
EnKa	42.5	**44.1**	47.5	49.1
EnTa	47.6	**48.0**	53.7	52.8
EnPe	**38.2**	–	68.3	–

Table 3: Official test results for standard DIRECTL+, and for non-standard JOINT with supplemental transliterations.

We observe many cases where the test results diverge from our development results. It appears that the provided development sets are not always representative of the final sets. To give some examples, the 2012 ArEn test set contains only a single space, as compared to 878 spaces present on the source side of the corresponding development set, while one-third of the target-side characters in the EnCh development set do not occur at all in the corresponding training set. In addition, the 2011 and 2012 test sets vary wildly in difficulty, as evidenced by the results in Table 2.

7 Conclusion

We found that simple linear combination of normalized confidence scores is an effective and robust method of system combination, although it is not guaranteed to improve upon the best base system. We also showed that a joint generation approach that directly leverages supplemental transliterations has the potential of boosting transliteration accuracy. However, the generality of these conclusions is limited by the narrow scope of the shared task and the deficiencies of the provided datasets.

Acknowledgments

This research was supported by the Natural Sciences and Engineering Research Council of Canada, and the Alberta Innovates – Technology Futures.

References

Aditya Bhargava and Grzegorz Kondrak. 2012. Leveraging supplemental representations for sequential transduction. In *Proceedings of the 2012 Conference of the North American Chapter of the Association for Computational Linguistics: Human Language Technologies*, pages 396–406, Montréal, Canada.

Aditya Bhargava, Bradley Hauer, and Grzegorz Kondrak. 2011. Leveraging transliterations from multiple languages. In *Proceedings of the 3rd Named Entities Workshop (NEWS 2011)*, pages 36–40, Chiang Mai, Thailand.

Maximilian Bisani and Hermann Ney. 2008. Joint-sequence models for grapheme-to-phoneme conversion. *Speech Communication*, 50(5):434–451.

Andrew Finch and Eiichiro Sumita. 2010. Transliteration using a phrase-based statistical machine translation system to re-score the output of a joint multigram model. In *Proceedings of the 2010 Named Entities Workshop*, pages 48–52, Uppsala, Sweden.

Sittichai Jiampojamarn, Grzegorz Kondrak, and Tarek Sherif. 2007. Applying many-to-many alignments and hidden markov models to letter-to-phoneme conversion. In *Human Language Technologies 2007: The Conference of the North American Chapter of the Association for Computational Linguistics; Proceedings of the Main Conference*, pages 372–379, Rochester, New York.

Sittichai Jiampojamarn, Colin Cherry, and Grzegorz Kondrak. 2008. Joint processing and discriminative training for letter-to-phoneme conversion. In *Proceedings of ACL-08: HLT*, pages 905–913, Columbus, Ohio.

Sittichai Jiampojamarn, Aditya Bhargava, Qing Dou, Kenneth Dwyer, and Grzegorz Kondrak. 2009. DirecTL: a language independent approach to transliteration. In *Proceedings of the 2009 Named Entities Workshop: Shared Task on Transliteration (NEWS 2009)*, pages 28–31, Suntec, Singapore.

Sittichai Jiampojamarn, Colin Cherry, and Grzegorz Kondrak. 2010a. Integrating joint n-gram features into a discriminative training framework. In *Human Language Technologies: The 2010 Annual Conference of the North American Chapter of the Association for Computational Linguistics*, pages 697–700, Los Angeles, California.

Sittichai Jiampojamarn, Kenneth Dwyer, Shane Bergsma, Aditya Bhargava, Qing Dou, Mi-Young Kim, and Grzegorz Kondrak. 2010b. Transliteration generation and mining with limited training resources. In *Proceedings of the 2010 Named Entities Workshop*, pages 39–47, Uppsala, Sweden.

Philipp Koehn, Hieu Hoang, Alexandra Birch, Chris Callison-Burch, Marcello Federico, Nicola Bertoldi, Brooke Cowan, Wade Shen, Christine Moran, Richard Zens, Chris Dyer, Ondrej Bojar, Alexandra Constantin, and Evan Herbst. 2007. Moses: Open source toolkit for statistical machine translation. In *Proceedings of the 45th Annual Meeting of the Association for Computational Linguistics Companion Volume Proceedings of the Demo and Poster Sessions*, pages 177–180, Prague, Czech Republic.

Grzegorz Kondrak, Xingkai Li, and Mohammad Salameh. 2012. Transliteration experiments on Chinese and Arabic. In *4th Named Entity Workshop (NEWS)*, pages 71–75, Jeju, Korea. System paper.

Keigo Kubo, Hiromichi Kawanami, Hiroshi Saruwatari, and Kiyohiro Shikano. 2011. Unconstrained many-to-many alignment for automatic pronunciation annotation. In *Asia-Pacific Signal and Information Processing Association Annual Summit and Conference (APSIPA ASC)*, Xi'an, China.

Najmeh Mousavi Nejad, Shahram Khadivi, and Kaveh Taghipour. 2011. The Amirkabir machine transliteration system for NEWS 2011: Farsi-to-English task. In *2011 Named Entities Workshop*, page 91.

Franz Josef Och and Hermann Ney. 2003. A systematic comparison of various statistical alignment models. *Computational Linguistics*, 29.

Franz Josef Och. 2003. Minimum error rate training in statistical machine translation. In *Proceedings of the 41st Annual Meeting of the Association for Computational Linguistics*, pages 160–167, Sapporo, Japan, July.

Yoh Okuno. 2012. Applying mpaligner to machine transliteration with Japanese-specific heuristics. In *Proceedings of the 4th Named Entity Workshop (NEWS) 2012*, pages 61–65, Jeju, Korea.

Kishore Papineni, Salim Roukos, Todd Ward, and Wei jing Zhu. 2002. BLEU: a method for automatic evaluation of machine translation. In *Proceedings of 40th Annual Meeting of the Association for Computational Linguistics*, pages 311–318.

Andreas Stolcke. 2002. SRILM - an extensible language modeling toolkit. In *Intl. Conf. Spoken Language Processing*, pages 901–904.

Chun-Kai Wu, Yu-Chun Wang, and Richard Tzong-Han Tsai. 2012. English-Korean named entity transliteration using substring alignment and reranking methods. In *Proceedings of the 4th Named Entity Workshop (NEWS) 2012*, pages 57–60, Jeju, Korea.

Lei Yao and Grzegorz Kondrak. 2015. Joint generation of transliterations from multiple representations. In *Proceedings of the 2015 Conference of the North American Chapter of the Association for Computational Linguistics: Human Language Technologies*, pages 943–952, Denver, Colorado.

Data representation methods and use of mined corpora for Indian language transliteration

Anoop Kunchukuttan **Pushpak Bhattacharyya**
Department of Computer Science and Engineering
Indian Institute of Technology Bombay
{anoopk,pb}@cse.iitb.ac.in

Abstract

Our NEWS 2015 shared task submission is a PBSMT based transliteration system with the following corpus preprocessing enhancements: (i) addition of word-boundary markers, and (ii) language-independent, overlapping character segmentation. We show that the addition of word-boundary markers improves transliteration accuracy substantially, whereas our overlapping segmentation shows promise in our preliminary analysis. We also compare transliteration systems trained using manually created corpora with the ones mined from parallel translation corpus for English to Indian language pairs. We identify the major errors in English to Indian language transliterations by analyzing heat maps of confusion matrices.

1 Introduction

Machine Transliteration can be viewed as a problem of transforming a sequence of characters in one alphabet to another. Transliteration can be seen as a special case of the general translation problem between two languages. The primary differences from the general translation problem are: (i) limited vocabulary size, and (ii) simpler grammar with no reordering. Phrase based statistical machine translation (PB-SMT) is a robust and well-understood technology and can be easily adopted for application to the transliteration problem (Noeman, 2009; Finch and Sumita, 2010). Our submission to the NEWS 2015 shared task is a PBSMT system. Over a baseline PBSMT system, we address two issues: (i) suitable data representation for training, and (ii) parallel transliteration corpus availability.

In many writing systems, the same logical/phonetic symbols can have different character representations depending on whether it occurs in initial, medial or terminal word position. For instance, Indian scripts have different characters for independent vowels and vowel diacritics. Independent vowels typically occurs at the beginning of the word, while diacritics occur in medial and terminal positions. The pronounciation, and hence the transliteration could also depend on the position of the characters. For instance, the terminal *ion* in *nation* would be pronounced differently from initial one in *ionize*. PBSMT learning of character sequence mappings is agnostic of the position of the character in the word. Hence, we explore to transform the data representation to encode position information. Zhang et al. (2012) did not report any benefit from such a representation for Chinese-English transliteration. We investigated if such encoding useful for alphabetic and consonantal scripts as opposed to logographic scripts like Chinese.

It is generally believed that syllabification of the text helps improve transliteration systems. However, syllabification systems are not available for all languages. Tiedemann (2012) proposed a character-level, overlapping bigram representation in the context of machine translation using transliteration. We can view this as weak, coarse and language independent syllabification approach. We explore this overlapping, segmentation approach for the transliteration task.

For many language pairs, parallel transliteration corpora are not publicly available. However, parallel translation corpora like Europarl (Koehn, 2005) and ILCI (Jha, 2012) are available for many language pairs. Transliteration corpora mined from such parallel corpora has been shown to be useful for machine translation, cross lingual information retrieval, etc. (Kunchukuttan et al., 2014). In this paper, we make an intrinsic evaluation of the performance of the automatically mined *BrahmiNet* transliteration corpus (Kunchukuttan et al.,

Proceedings of the Fifth Named Entity Workshop, joint with 53rd ACL and the 7th IJCNLP, pages 78–82,
Beijing, China, July 26-31, 2015. ©2015 Association for Computational Linguistics

2015) for transliteration between English and Indian languages. The *BrahmiNet* corpus contains transliteration corpora for 110 Indian language pairs mined from the ILCI corpus, a parallel translation corpora of 11 Indian languages (Jha, 2012).

The rest of the paper is organized as follows. Section 2 and Section 3 describes our system and experimental setup respectively. Section 4 discusses the results of various data representation methods and the use of mined corpus respectively. Section 5 concludes the report.

2 System Description

We use a standard PB-SMT model for transliteration between the various language pairs. It is a discriminative, log-linear model which uses standard SMT features *viz.* direct/inverse phrase translation probabilities, direct/inverse lexical translation probabilities, phrase penalty, word penalty and language model score. The feature weights are tuned to optimize BLEU (Papineni et al., 2002) using the Minimum Error Rate Training algorithm (Och, 2003). It would be better to explore optimizing metrics like accuracy or edit distance instead of using BLEU as a proxy for these metrics. We experiment with various transliteration units as discussed in Section 2.1. We use a 5-gram language model over the transliteration units estimated using Witten-Bell smoothing. Since transliteration does not require any reordering, monotone decoding was done.

2.1 Data Representation

We create different transliteration models based on different basic transliteration units in the source and target training corpus. We use character (P) as well as bigram representations (T). In character based system, the character is the basic unit of transliteration. In bigram-based system, the overlapping bigram is the basic unit of transliteration. We also augmented the word representation with word boundary markers (M) (^ for start of word and $ end of word). The various representations we experimented with are illustrated below:

character (P)	H I N D I
character+boundary marker (M)	^ H I N D I $
bigram (T)	HI IN ND DI I
bigram+boundary marker (M+T)	^H HI IN ND DI I$ $

The abbreviations mentioned above are used subsequently to refer to these data representations.

2.2 Use of mined transliteration corpus

We explore the use of transliteration corpora mined from translation corpora for transliteration. Sajjad et al. (2012) proposed an unsupervised method for mining transliteration pairs from parallel corpus. Their approach models parallel translation corpus generation as a generative process comprising an interpolation of a transliteration and a non-transliteration process. The parameters of the generative process are learnt using the EM procedure, followed by extraction of transliteration pairs from the parallel corpora by setting an appropriate threshold. We compare the quality of the transliteration systems built from such mined corpora with systems trained on manually created NEWS 2015 corpora for English-Indian language pairs.

3 Experimental Setup

For building the transliteration model with the NEWS 2015 shared task corpus as well as the *BrahmiNet* corpus, we used 500 word pairs for tuning and the rest for SMT training. The experimental results are reported on the NEWS 2015 development sets in both cases. The details of the NEWS 2015 shared task datasets are mentioned in shared text report, while the size of the *BrahmiNet* datasets are listed below:

Src	Tgt	Size
En	Hi	10513
En	Ba	7567
En	Ta	3549

We use the *Moses* toolkit (Koehn et al., 2007) to train the transliteration system and the language models were estimated using the SRILM toolkit (Stolcke and others, 2002). The transliteration pairs are mined using the transliteration module in *Moses* (Durrani et al., 2014).

4 Results and Error Analysis

4.1 Effect of Data Representation methods

Table 1 shows transliteration results for various data representation methods on the development set. We see improvements in transliteration accuracy of upto 18% due to the use of word-boundary markers. The MRR also shows an improvement of upto 15%. An analysis of improvement for the En-Hi pair shows that a major reason for the improve-

Src	Tgt	Top-1 Accuracy				F-score				MRR			
		P	M	T	M+T	P	M	T	M+T	P	M	T	M+T
En	Ka	27.6	32.7	28.9	30.4	83.44	85.38	84.75	85.61	39.03	45.15	41.3	41.92
En	Ta	28.6	32.4	31.4	33.4	85.44	86.73	86.64	87.38	41.06	44.89	42.76	45.11
En	Hi	38.82	41.02	37.01	40.52	86.02	86.62	85.77	86.72	51.19	53.28	47.68	51.1
En	He	54.6	56.4	54.4	54.5	91.68	92.29	91.7	91.49	67.68	68.06	64.5	63.76
En	Ba	35.4	38.24	34.48	36.41	86.15	87.13	86	86.78	48.84	51.58	46.56	48.46
Th	En	31.44	32.2	29.64	30.34	84.79	85.09	84.01	84.17	42.6	43.98	40.63	40.48
En	Pe	53.5	57.8	53.3	56.65	91.93	92.76	92.02	92.78	66.58	70.42	64.91	67.66
Ch	En	11.66	10.74	5.33	4.82	72.94	72.33	60.35	61.15	17.95	16.94	8.54	7.52

Table 1: Results on NEWS 2015 development set (in %)

Src	Tgt	P	T
En	Ka	17	25.1
En	Ta	15.3	27.1
En	Hi	27.28	32.3
En	Ba	27.79	32.05
En	He	47.9	54.6
En	Pe	39.35	48.8

Table 2: Top-1 accuracy on NEWS 2015 development set without tuning (in %)

ment seems to the correct generation of vowel diacritics (*maatraa*). Word boundary markers also reduce the following errors: (i) missing initial vowels, (ii) wrong consonants in the initial and final syllable, and (iii) incorrect or spurious generation of *halanta* (inherent vowel suppressor) character. Some examples of these corrections are shown below:

Src	P	M
KALYARI	कालयारी (kAlayArI)	कल्यारी (kalyArI)
NAHAR	नेहर (nehara)	नाहर (nAhara)
AHILYAA	हिल्या (hilyA)	अहिल्या (ahilyA)
AVEDIS	वेडिस (veDisa)	एवेडिस (eveDisa)
AVEDIS	कीर्तपुर (kIrtapura)	कीरतपुर (kIratapura)

We also tried to identify the major errors in English to Indian languages using heat maps of the character-level confusion matrices (Figure 1 shows one for En-Hi). We observed that the following errors are common across all English-Indian language pairs in the shared task: (i) incorrect generation of vowel diacritics, especially confusion between long and short vowels, (ii) *schwa* deletion, (iii) confusion between dental and retroflex consonants, (iv) incorrect or spurious generation of *halanta* (inherent vowel suppressor) character as well as the *aakar maatra* (vowel diacritic for आ(aa)). Hi and Ba show confusion between sibilants (स,श,ष), while Ta and Ka exhibits incorrect or spurious generation of य (ya).

However, the use of a overlapping bigram representation does not show any significant improvement in results over the baseline output. The above results are for systems tuned to maximize BLEU. However, BLEU does not seem the most intuitive tuning metric for the the bigram representation. Hence, we compare the untuned output results (shown in Table 2 for a few language pairs). As we anticipated, we found that the bigram representation gave a significant improvement in accuracy (on an average of about 25%). The combination of word-boundary marker and bigram representation performs best. This suggests the need to tune the SMT system to an alternative metric like edit distance so that the benefit of bigram representation can be properly harnessed. The following is an example where bigram representation resulted in the correct generation of consonants, where the character representation made errors:

Src	P	T
DABHADE	दाबहादे (dAbahAde)	दाभाडे (dAbhADe)

4.2 Transliteration using an automatically mined corpus

Table 3 shows results on the development set when trained using the *BrahmiNet* corpus. The top-1 accuracy is less as compared to training on the NEWS 2015 training corpus. The accuracy very low compared to NEWS 2015 training for Tamil,

Src	Tgt	Accuracy	F-score	MRR
En	Hi	28.39	82.66	39.73
En	Ba	20.59	79.45	30.69
En	Ta	9.3	74.75	15.25

Table 3: Results with BrahmiNet training on NEWS 2105 dev set (in %)

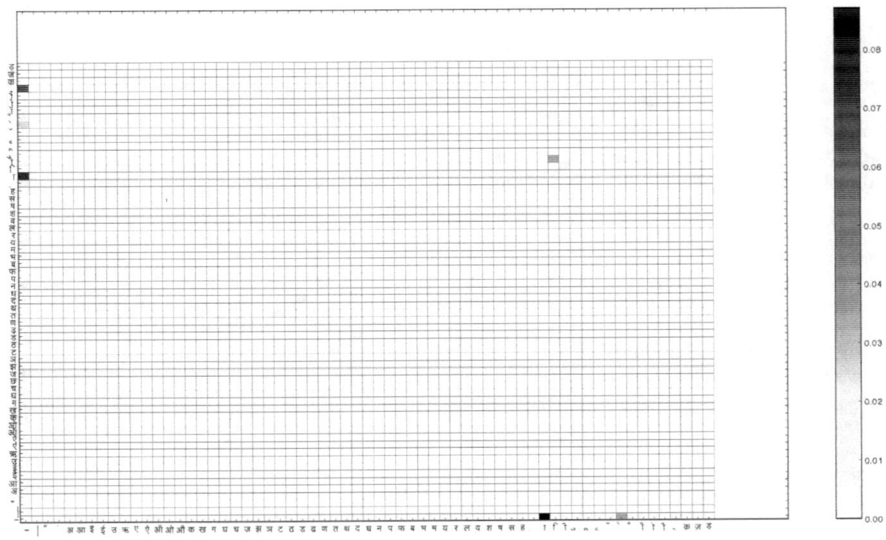

Figure 1: Heat Map for En-Hi (marker, news_2015) system. Color in cell indicates proportion of errors (y-axis: reference set, x-axis: hypothesis set)

where the quality of mined corpus suffers on account of the presence of suffixes due to the agglutinative nature of the language. This results in some wrongly mined pairs as well as smaller number of word pairs being mined. The F-score does not suffer as much as top-1 accuracy and all languages have an F-score greater than 70%. The MRR suggests that the correct transliteration can be found in the top 3 candidates for Hi and Ba, and in the top-7 candidates for Ta. This shows that though the top-1 accuracy of the system is lower than a manually generated corpus, the use of the top-k candidates can be useful in downstream applications like machine translation and cross lingual IR. Since the NEWS 2015 corpus is larger than the *BrahmiNet* corpus, we train a random subset of the NEWS 2015 corpus of the same size as the *BrahmiNet* corpus. In addition, we also experiment with stricter selection thresholds in the mining process.

Since, NEWS 2015 development corpus is quite similar to the NEWS training corpus, we use another corpus (Gupta et al., 2012) to evaluate both the systems. In all these cases, the NEWS corpus gave superior accuracy as compared to *BrahmiNet*. To explain the superiority of the NEWS corpus over all the configurations, we computed the average entropy for the conditional transliteration probability (Chinnakotla et al., 2010). The average entropy for the P(En|Hi) distribution at the character level is higher for the *BrahmiNet* corpus (0.8) as compared to the NEWS 2015 corpus (0.574). The same observation is seen for the P(Hi|En) distribution. This means that there is a higher ambiguity in selecting transliteration in the *BrahmiNet* corpus.

5 Conclusion

We addressed data representation and availability issues in PBSMT based transliteration, with a special focus on English-Indian language pairs. We showed that adding boundary markers to the word representation helps to significantly improve the transliteration accuracy. We also noted that the an overlapping character segmentation can be useful subject to optimizing the appropriate evaluation metrics for transliteration systems. We show that though automatically mined corpora provided lower top-1 transliteration accuracy, the top-10 accuracy, MRR and F-score are competitive to justify the use of the top-k candidates from these mined corpora for translation and IR systems.

References

Manoj Chinnakotla, Om Damani, and Avijit Satoskar. 2010. Transliteration for resource-scarce languages. *ACM Transactions on Asian Language Information Processing (TALIP)*.

Nadir Durrani, Hieu Hoang, Philipp Koehn, and Hassan Sajjad. 2014. Integrating an Unsupervised Transliteration Model into Statistical Machine Translation. *EACL 2014*.

Andrew M Finch and Eiichiro Sumita. 2010. A bayesian model of bilingual segmentation for transliteration. In *IWSLT*.

Kanika Gupta, Monojit Choudhury, and Kalika Bali. 2012. Mining hindi-english transliteration pairs from online hindi lyrics. In *LREC*, pages 2459--2465.

Girish Nath Jha. 2012. The TDIL program and the Indian Language Corpora Initiative. In *Language Resources and Evaluation Conference*.

Philipp Koehn, Hieu Hoang, Alexandra Birch, Chris Callison-Burch, Marcello Federico, Nicola Bertoldi, Brooke Cowan, Wade Shen, Christine Moran, Richard Zens, et al. 2007. Moses: Open source toolkit for statistical machine translation. In *Proceedings of the 45th Annual Meeting of the ACL on Interactive Poster and Demonstration Sessions*, pages 177--180. Association for Computational Linguistics.

Philipp Koehn. 2005. Europarl: A parallel corpus for statistical machine translation. In *MT summit*, volume 5, pages 79--86.

Anoop Kunchukuttan, Ratish Pudupully, Rajen Chatterjee, Abhijit Mishra, and Pushpak Bhattacharyya. 2014. The IIT Bombay SMT System for ICON 2014 Tools Contest. In *NLP Tools Contest at ICON 2014*.

Anoop Kunchukuttan, Ratish Puduppully, and Pushpak Bhattacharyya. 2015. Brahmi-Net: A transliteration and script conversion system for languages of the Indian subcontinent. In *Conference of the North American Chapter of Association for Computational Linguistics: System Demonstrations*.

Sara Noeman. 2009. Language independent transliteration system using phrase based smt approach on substrings. In *Proceedings of the 2009 Named Entities Workshop: Shared Task on Transliteration*.

Franz Josef Och. 2003. Minimum error rate training in statistical machine translation. In *Proceedings of the 41st Annual Meeting on Association for Computational Linguistics-Volume 1*.

Kishore Papineni, Salim Roukos, Todd Ward, and Wei-Jing Zhu. 2002. Bleu: a method for automatic evaluation of machine translation. In *Proceedings of the 40th annual meeting on association for computational linguistics*, pages 311--318. Association for Computational Linguistics.

Hassan Sajjad, Alexander Fraser, and Helmut Schmid. 2012. A statistical model for unsupervised and semi-supervised transliteration mining. In *Proceedings of the 50th Annual Meeting of the Association for Computational Linguistics*.

Andreas Stolcke et al. 2002. Srilm-an extensible language modeling toolkit. In *INTERSPEECH*.

Jörg Tiedemann. 2012. Character-based pivot translation for under-resourced languages and domains. In *Proceedings of the 13th Conference of the European Chapter of the Association for Computational Linguistics*, pages 141--151. Association for Computational Linguistics.

Chunyue Zhang, Tingting Li, and Tiejun Zhao. 2012. Syllable-based machine transliteration with extra phrase features. In *Proceedings of the 4th Named Entity Workshop*.

NCU IISR English-Korean and English-Chinese Named Entity Transliteration Using Different Grapheme Segmentation Approaches

Yu-Chun Wang[†] **Chun-Kai Wu**[‡] **Richard Tzong-Han Tsai**[§*]

[†]Department of Computer Science and Information Engineering, National Taiwan University, Taiwan
[‡]Department of Computer Science, National Tsinghua University, Taiwan
[§]Department of Computer Science and Information Engineering, National Central University, Taiwan

d97023@csie.ntu.edu.tw s102065512@m102.nthu.edu.tw
thtsai@csie.ncu.edu.tw

Abstract

This paper describes our approach to English-Korean and English-Chinese transliteration task of NEWS 2015. We use different grapheme segmentation approaches on source and target languages to train several transliteration models based on the M2M-aligner and DirecTL+, a string transduction model. Then, we use two reranking techniques based on string similarity and web co-occurrence to select the best transliteration among the prediction results from the different models. Our English-Korean standard and non-standard runs achieve 0.4482 and 0.5067 in top-1 accuracy respectively, and our English-Chinese standard runs achieves 0.2925 in top-1 accuracy.

1 Introduction

Named entity translation is a key problem in many NLP research fields such as machine translation, cross-language information retrieval, and question answering. The vast majority of named entities (NE) such as person or organization names do not appear in bilingual dictionaries, and new NEs are being generated every day, making it difficult to keep an up-to-date list of NEs. One solution for NE translation is to use online encyclopedias like Wikipedia that contain pages in both the source and target language. However, coverage is spotty for many languages and/or NE categories.

Since the translations of many NEs are based on transliteration, a method of mapping phonemes or graphemes from a source language to a target language, researchers have developed automated transliteration techniques to add to the NE translation toolbox. NE transliteration has featured as a shared task in previous Named Entities Workshops (NEWS).

In the shared task for NEWS 2015, we focus on English-Korean and English-Chinese transliteration. We adopt the M2M-aligner and DirecTL+ to map substrings and predict transliteration results. Jiampojamarn et al. (2010) achieved promising results using this approach in the NEWS 2010 transliteration task. The Korean writing system, Hangul, is alphabetic, but Chinese characters are logograms. Because English and Korean use alphabetic writing systems, we apply different grapheme segmentation methods to create several transliteration models. For Chinese, we treat each distinct Chinese character as a basic unit for the alignment step. In order to improve the transliteration performance, we also apply two ranking techniques to select the best transliterations.

This paper is organized as follows. In Section 2 we describe our main approach, including how we preprocess the data, our alignment and training methods, and our reranking techniques. In Section 3 we show our results on the English-Korean and English-Chinese transliteration tasks and discuss our findings. Finally the conclusion is in Section 4.

2 Our Approach

Our approach for English-Korean and English-Chinese transliteration comprises the following steps:

1. Preprocessing
2. Alignment
3. DirecTL+ training
4. Re-ranking results

*corresponding author

Proceedings of the Fifth Named Entity Workshop, joint with 53rd ACL and the 7th IJCNLP, pages 83–87,
Beijing, China, July 26-31, 2015. ©2015 Association for Computational Linguistics

2.1 Preprocessing

2.1.1 English

Since English uses the Latin alphabet, we use three different segmentation methods for alignment: single letter, fine segmentation algorithm, and phonemic representation.

Single Letter (SINGLE) NEs are separated into single letters for further alignment. For example, the English name “ALEXANDER” is separated as four letters “A L E X A N D E R” for the alignment in the next step.

Fine-grained Segment Algorithm (FSA) Unlike English letters and words, each Hangul block or Chinese character corresponds to a syllable. Some previous approaches have used English letters and Chinese characters/Korean syllabic blocks as the basic alignment units for transliteration (Oh and Choi, 2006; Li et al., 2004; Jia et al., 2009). Other approaches have tried to segment English NEs into syllabic chunks for alignment with Hangul blocks or Chinese characters (Wan and Verspoor, 1998; Jiang et al., 2007; Zhang et al., 2012).

We adopt a heuristic syllable segmentation algorithm, namely Fine-grained Segment Algorithm (FSA), proposed by Zhang et al. (2012) with slight modification to syllabify English NEs. Our modified version of the FSA is defined as follows:

1. Replace ‘*x*’ in English names with ‘*k s*’.
2. {‘*a*’, ‘*o*’, ‘*e*’, ‘*i*’, ‘*u*’} are defined as vowels. ‘*y*’ is defined as a vowel when it is not followed by a vowel.
3. When ‘*w*’ follows ‘*a*’, ‘*e*’, ‘*o*’ and isn’t followed by ‘*h*’, treat ‘*w*’ and the preceding vowel as a new vowel symbol; Step 2 and 3 form the basic vowel set.
4. A consecutive vowels sequence which is formed by the basic vowel set is treated as a new vowel symbol, excepting ‘*iu*’, ‘*eo*’, ‘*io*’, ‘*oi*’, ‘*ia*’, ‘*ui*’, ‘*ua*’, ‘*uo*’; Step 2, 3 and 4 form the new vowel set.
5. Consecutive consonants are separated; a vowel symbol(in the new vowel set) followed by a consonant sequence is separated from the sequence; if a vowel followed by a consonat sequence and the first consonat is { ‘*h*’, ‘*l*’, ‘*m*’, ‘*n*’, ‘*r*’ }, the first consonat symbol is concatenated with the vowel into a syllable.
6. A consonant and its following vowel are treated as a syllable; the rest of the isolated consonants and vowels are regarded as individual syllables in each word.

   For example, the English term “ALEXANDER” is segmented as “A LE K SAN DER” by the FSA.

Phonemic Representation (PHONEME) In addition, since Korean is a phonological writing system, for non-standard runs, we also adopt phonemic information for English name entities. The English word pronunciations are obtained from the CMU Pronouncing Dictionary v0.7a. The CMU pronouncing dictionary provides the phonemic representations of English pronunciations with a sequence of phoneme symbols. For instance, the previous example *ALEXANDER* is segmented and tagged as the phonemic representation $<$ AE L AH G Z AE N D ER $>$. Since the CMU pronouncing dictionary does not cover all the pronunciation information of the name entities in the training data, we also apply LOGIOS Lexicon Tool to generate the phonemic representations of all other name entities not in the CMU pronouncing dictionary.

2.1.2 Korean

Korean writing system, namely *Hangul*, is alphabetical. However, unlike western writing system with Latin alphabets, Korean alphabet is composed into syllabic blocks. Each Korean syllabic block represents a syllable which has three components: initial consonant, medial vowel and optionally final consonant. Korean has 14 initial consonants, 10 medial vowels, and 7 final consonants. For instance, the syllabic block “신” (sin) is composed with three letters: a initial consonant “ㅅ” (s), a medial vowel ㅑ” (i), and a final consonant “ㄴ” (n).

We take two segmentation method for Korean: Hangul blocks and romanized letters.

Hangul Blocks (HANGUL) Hangul syllabic blocks of Korean words are separated into single blocks for further alignment. For example, the

http://www.speech.cs.cmu.edu./cgi-bin/cmudict

http://www.speech.cs.cmu.edu/tools/lextool.html

Korean word "녹스" is separated as two syllabic blocks "녹 스" for the alignment in the next step.

Romanized Letters (ROMAN) This segmentation method break each Hangul syllabic blocks into Korean letters and then convert these Korean letters into Roman letters according to Revised Romanization of Korean for convenient processing. For example, the Korean word "녹스" is first taken apart as "ㄴ ㅗ ㄱ ㅅ ㅡ", and then romanized as "n o k s eu".

2.1.3 Chinese

For Chinese, we treat each Chinese character as a basic alignment unit. Chinese chacters of a Chinese word are segment as each single Chinese character for further alignment processing. For example, the Chinese word "诺克斯" is separated as three character "诺 克 斯".

2.2 Alignment

After generating English, Korean, and Chinese segmented substrings in the previous step, we determine the alignment between each English-Korean and English-Chinese pair using the M2M-aligner (Jiampojamarn et al., 2007). The M2M-aligner is a many-to-many alignment method based on the expectation maximization (EM) algorithm. It allows us to create alignments between substrings of various lengths. During alignment, empty strings (*nulls*) are only allowed on the target side.

2.3 DirecTL+ Training

With aligned English-Korean and English-Chinese pairs, we can train our transliteration model. We apply DirecTL+ (Jiampojamarn et al., 2008) for training and testing. DirecTL+ is an online discriminative training model for string transduction problems. We individually train the transliteration models with different segmentation methods individually mentioned in section 2.1.

2.4 Reranking Results

Because we train several transliteration models with different alignment settings, we can combine the results from different models to select the best transliterations. Therefore, reranking is a necessary step to generate thc final results. For reranking, we propose two approaches.

1. Orthography Similarity Ranking
2. Web-based Ranking

2.4.1 Orthography Similarity Ranking

For standard runs which are allowed to use the training data only, we measure the orthographic similarity between the term in the source language and the transliteration candidate. The transliteration candidates in target languages are all first Romanized into Latin alphabet sequences. Then, we rank the similarity between the source language term and the Romanized transliteration candidate according to the string edit distance.

2.4.2 Web-based Ranking

The second reranking method is based on the occurrence of transliterations in the web corpora. We send each transliteration pair generated by our transliteration models to the Bing web search engine to get the co-occurrence count of the pair in the retrieval results. We use mutual information between the source language term and the transliteration candidate as the similarity score for ranking.

3 Results

To measure the transliteration models with different segmentation methods and the reranking methods, we construct the following experimental runs:

English-Korean (EnKo) Runs:

- Run 1: SINGLE + HANGUL
- Run 2: SINGLE + ROMAN
- Run 3: PHONEME + ROMAN
- Run 4: FSA + HANGUL
- Run 5: FSA + ROMAN
- Run 6: Orthography Similarity Ranking with Run 1 to 5
- Run 7: Web-based Ranking with Run 1 to 5

English-Chinese (EnCh) Runs:

- Run 1: FSA + Chinese characters
- Run 2: SINGLE + Chinese characters

Table 1 and table 2 show the final results of our transliteration approaches on the English-Korean (EnKo) and the English-Chinese (EnCh) test data.

The EnKo results show that the alignment between single English letter and Romanized Korean letter (Run 2) achieves the best results among run 1

Table 1: Final results on the English-Korean (EnKo) test data

Run	NEWS 11				NEWS12			
	ACC	F-score	MRR	MAP_{ref}	ACC	F-score	MRR	MAP_{ref}
1	0.3186	0.6576	0.3186	0.3112	0.3276	0.7078	0.3276	0.3269
2	0.4483	0.7255	0.4483	0.4392	0.4457	0.7482	0.4457	0.4448
3	0.2742	0.6000	0.2742	0.2689	0.1457	0.5222	0.1457	0.1455
4	0.2151	0.5707	0.2151	0.2098	0.1743	0.5835	0.1743	0.1740
5	0.0427	0.3329	0.0427	0.0415	0.0562	0.3752	0.0562	0.0562
6	0.2085	0.5270	0.3432	0.2048	0.1952	0.5522	0.3349	0.1950
7	0.4992	0.7330	0.5395	0.4943	0.5067	0.7614	0.5317	0.5055

Table 2: Final results on the English-Chinese (EnCh) test data

Run	NEWS 11				NEWS12			
	ACC	F-score	MRR	MAP_{ref}	ACC	F-score	MRR	MAP_{ref}
1	0.2325	0.6303	0.2325	0.2199	0.2351	0.6237	0.2351	0.2242
2	0.2925	0.6719	0.2925	0.2772	0.2798	0.6455	0.2798	0.2652

to 5. The run with the alignment between English phonemic representation and Romanized Korean letter (Run 3) is not as good as Run 2. It might be due to two reasons: one is that the Korean transliteration is often based on the orthography, not the actual pronunciation; the second reason is that the pronunciation from LOGIOS lexicon tool may not be accurate to get the correct phonemic forms.

The FSA segmentation method (Run 4 and 5) does not perform well as other runs, especially, the Run 5 (FSA + ROMAN) has the worst result. The reason might be the unbalanced segment units between English and Korean. The M2M-aligner is originally designed to do letter-to-phoneme alignment. The FSA method grouping the consecutive English letter into syllables, but the Romanized Korean letters are all single characters. It might cause the M2M-aligner generate the incorrect alignment in this run. In EnCh runs, the FSA segmentation method (Run 1) also performs slightly worse than the single English letter segmentation method (Run 2).

The web-based ranking method (EnKo Run 7) significantly improves the transliteration performance. Because web corpora contains the actual usages of the transliterations, it is a good resource to rank and select the best transliterations. The orthography similarity ranking method (Run 6) does not improve but actually degrades the transliteration performance. This may be because the English orthography does not always reflect actual pronunciations; therefore, the similarity between English and Korean orthographies is insufficient to measure the quality of transliteration candidates.

4 Conclusion

In this paper, we describe our approach to English-Korean and English-Chinese NE transliteration task for NEWS 2015. We adopt different grapheme segmentation methods for the source and target languages. For English, three segmentation methods are used: single letter, fine-grained syllable algorithm, and phonemic representation. For Korean, we segment according to Hangul syllabic blocks and Romanized Hangul letters. For Chinese, we treat each Chinese character as a basic alignment unit. After segmenting the training data, we use the M2M-aligner to get the alignments from the source and target languages. Next, we train different transliteration models based on DirecTL+ with the alignments from the M2M-aligner. Finally, we use two reranking methods: web-based ranking using the Bing search engine, and the orthography similarity method based on the string edit distance of the orthographic forms in source and target languages. In experiments, our method achieves accuracy up to 0.4483 in the standard run and 0.5067 in the non-standard run for English-Korean. For English-Chinese standard run, it achieves an accuracy of 0.2925.

References

Yuxiang Jia, Danqing Zhu, and Shiwen Yu. 2009. A noisy channel model for grapheme-based machine transliteration. In *Proceedings of the 2009 Named Entities Workshop: Shared Task on Transliteration*, pages 88–91. Association for Computational Linguistics.

Sittichai Jiampojamarn, Grzegorz Kondrak, and Tarek Sherif. 2007. Applying many-to-many alignments and hidden markov models to letter-to-phoneme conversion. In *Human Language Technologies 2007: The Conference of the North American Chapter of the Association for Computational Linguistics; Proceedings of the Main Conference*, pages 372–379, Rochester, New York, April. Association for Computational Linguistics.

Sittichai Jiampojamarn, Colin Cherry, and Grzegorz Kondrak. 2008. Joint processing and discriminative training for letter-to-phoneme conversion. In *Proceedings of ACL-08: HLT*, pages 905–913, Columbus, Ohio, June. Association for Computational Linguistics.

Sittichai Jiampojamarn, Colin Cherry, and Grzegorz Kondrak. 2010. Integrating joint n-gram features into a discriminative training framework. In *Proceedings of NAACL-2010*, Los Angeles, CA, June. Association for Computational Linguistics.

Long Jiang, Ming Zhou, Lee-Feng Chien, and Cheng Niu. 2007. Named entity translation with web mining and transliteration. In *IJCAI*, volume 7, pages 1629–1634.

Haizhou Li, Min Zhang, and Jian Su. 2004. A joint source-channel model for machine transliteration. In *Proceedings of the 42nd Annual Meeting on association for Computational Linguistics*, page 159. Association for Computational Linguistics.

Jong-Hoon Oh and Key-Sun Choi. 2006. An ensemble of transliteration models for information retrieval. *Information processing & management*, 42(4):980–1002.

Stephen Wan and Cornelia Maria Verspoor. 1998. Automatic english-chinese name transliteration for development of multilingual resources. In *Proceedings of the 17th international conference on Computational linguistics-Volume 2*, pages 1352–1356. Association for Computational Linguistics.

Chunyue Zhang, Tingting Li, and Tiejun Zhao. 2012. Syllable-based machine transliteration with extrac phrase features. In *Proceedings of NEWS 2012*, pages 52–56.

Author Index